PETER DAWKINS

Shakespeare's Wisdom
in
The Tempest

The Wisdom of Shakespeare Series

I. C. Media Productions

Published by I C Media Productions
Warwickshire, United Kingdom

ISBN 0-9532890-3-6

Design & Typeset by Starnine Design

Printed in Great Britain by Biddles Limited,
Guildford and Kings Lynn.

The Wisdom of Shakespeare Series

Other Titles in the Series

About the Author

Peter Dawkins was educated at King Edward's High School, Birmingham, and St Catharine's College, Cambridge. He practised as an architect for ten years in both England and Scotland, until 1978, when he set out to devote himself full-time to research and educational work in connection with the world's wisdom traditions, mythology, sacred architecture and sacred landscape.

Peter is especially involved in pioneering work in Zoence, a Western equivalent to the Chinese Feng-Shui, and with the Neoplatonic and Rosicrucian foundations of modern science and society. Author of many books, he teaches internationally through lectures and workshops, and by taking people on special journeys or pilgrimages to sacred sites of the world. He has studied Shakespeare deeply, and has given Shakespeare seminars and workshops for over fifteen years. He is an advisor to actors, directors and theatre companies, including the Globe Theatre, London.

Peter lives in Warwickshire with his wife Sarah and three children.

Dedication

This book I dedicate to the memory of FT.

Acknowledgements

I would like to thank all my friends who have helped make this book possible, and in particular the following people: the 'Roses' team who have assisted me, edited, illustrated, and helped design and prepare the book for publishing—my wife Sarah, my sons John and Samuel, Anne McQueen Johnston and Michèle Beaufoy; my 'professional' friends who have given me encouragement, information and ideas—especially Mark Rylance (actor and Artistic Director of the Shakespeare Globe Theatre) and his wife Claire Van Kampen (Director of Music and Artistic Assistant of the Shakespeare Globe Theatre), whose 1991 Phoebus Cart production of *The Tempest* was so memorable, and Hugh Young (playwright and actor-director of Daylight Theatre); and my 'supportive' friends who have helped provide the means—Gay Browning, Mary Perry, Mary Pout and Diana Tinson.

Illustrations

Cover illustration, chapter headpieces and tailpieces by Michèle Beaufoy.

Map by John Dawkins.

Photograph of author by Marianne Rieke.

Illustration 5 based on Mountain High Map images (Mountain High Maps® Copyright © 1993 Digital Wisdom, Inc.).

Illustration 6 reproduced from Man the Grand Symbol of the Mysteries by Manly P. Hall, published by the Philosophical Research Society, Los Angeles.

Illustration 9 reproduced by permission of the British Library (8675139.G1118).

Illustration 15 reproduced by permission of the British Library (12305.BBB.36).

Illustration 16 reproduced by permission of the British Library (C.48.a.18p19).

Textual Note

All quotations from Shakespeare's *The Tempest* are taken from the Arden Shakespeare, edited by Frank Kermode (1954). All quotations from the Bible are taken from The Companion Bible (1974), being the Authorised Version of 1611 as published by the Revisers in their 'Parallel Bible' in 1885.

Contents

Illustrations

Introduction

The 'Wisdom of Shakespeare' Series

This series on the Wisdom of Shakespeare is designed to investigate and make known the extraordinary wisdom, knowledge and philosophy contained in the Shakespeare plays.

Besides the plays themselves, a clue to the greatness of Shakespeare in this respect is given by Ben Jonson in his tribute to the Author prefacing the Shakespeare 1st Folio of 1623, as also by the inscription on the contemporaneous Shakespeare Monument.

On the Shakespeare Monument, erected *c.* 1620-23 in Holy Trinity Church at Stratford-upon-Avon, Warwickshire, to honour the memory of Shakespeare, the great Bard is referred to (in Latin) as 'A Pylus in judgment, a Socrates in genius, a Maro in art'.

Pylus was the appellation of Nestor, King of Pylus, one of the Argonauts who went in search of the Golden Fleece and who was the most perfect of Homer's heroes in the Trojan War. As a statesman, ruler and judge, Pylus was renowned for his eloquence, address, wisdom, justice and prudence of mind.

Socrates was the most celebrated philosopher of Greece and a renowned orator. The Delphic Oracle proclaimed him as the wisest of mankind. He was the principal instigator of the great philosophies that have constituted the major traditions of Western civilisation, and was the advocate of clarity and the inductive procedure, for which he was particularly famed. His great aim was the happiness and good of his countrymen, and the reformation of their corrupted morals. By introducing moral philosophy, he induced people to consider themselves, their passions, their opinions, their duties, faculties and actions. He used drama to aid him in this, and the tragedies attributed to his pupil Euripides are said to have been at least partly composed by him, although he remained hidden as a playwright behind the mask of his pupil.

Maro was the surname of Virgil, the greatest of the Roman poets. He was known as the prince of poets and Homer's successor. He was not only a highly learned scholar and refined writer, but also a high initiate of the Orphic Mysteries as practised at Naples, where he lived for the last part of his life. His *Æneid* was based upon the Mysteries and Homer's epic tales, the *Iliad* and *Odyssey*.

For Shakespeare to be likened to these three illustrious men—not just one, but all three—is an enormous compliment and says a great deal about the Bard.

This viewpoint is supported by Ben Jonson, a renowned playwright and poet in his own right. In his tributary poem to Shakespeare prefacing the Shakespeare 1st Folio, Jonson refers to his 'beloved' friend as an Apollo and Mercury, and as the 'Sweet Swan of Avon'. Furthermore, implying that Shakespeare was, like him, a noted classical scholar, he declares in his tribute that even if Shakespeare had small Latin and less Greek, he (Ben) would still honour him, calling forth the great Roman and Greek tragedians to hear and applaud his tragedies. As for comedies, Ben can think of no one of the ancient Greeks or Romans who even approaches Shakespeare: he is alone, supreme.

To be likened to the gods Apollo and Mercury, rather than just inspired by them, is a mighty tribute, particularly as coming from the talented and critical poet laureate, Ben Jonson. Apollo is the god of poetic inspiration and illumination, and leader of the choir of Muses. Mercury is the god of eloquence and learning.

The 'sweet swan' is a reference to the singing swan, which is sweetest when singing its own 'swan-song'. This was the symbol of Orpheus, musician to the Argonauts and the originator of the Orphic Mysteries that subsequently became the wisdom teachings and Mysteries of Classical Greece and Rome. These Mysteries formed a foundation of Classical philosophy and of all Platonic and Neoplatonic thought. Orpheus was considered to be the representative of Bacchus, the god of Drama, whose drama was in particular the Mysteries that were performed by the bacchants, bacchantes and *eumolpoi* ('good singers'), the initiates and hierophants of the Orphic Mysteries. Both comedy and tragedy, and theatre as such, derive from the Bacchanalian Mysteries. Moreover, the white swan, symbol of Orpheus and the *Eumolpoi,* is an emblem of Apollo.

Mercury (Roman *Mercurius*) is derived from the Ancient Egyptian *Maa Kheru,* meaning 'the True Word' and 'he who is of true voice'. It was a title bestowed on the high initiates of the Egyptian Mysteries—*i.e.* those who had sung their 'swan-song' and undergone psychological death and rebirth,—a title which was still used in the Classical Mysteries. Another Greek name for Mercury was Hermes Trismegistus (*i.e.* Hermes the Thrice Greatest), but this title was applied specifically to the greatest of all the initiates in any epoch. From this name comes the term 'Hermetic' for the great wisdom teachings and developing philosophical thought that have been handed on from the time of the Ancient Egyptians to successive generations and cultures, and of which we are inheritors today via the Neoplatonism of the Renaissance and the great poetry of Shakespeare.

The works of Shakespeare declare him to be one of the greatest, if not *the* greatest, of the Neoplatonists. His plays are suffused with Renaissance Neoplatonism. To understand this is to understand Shakespeare.

Renaissance Neoplatonism

The founders of Renaissance Neoplatonism were Marsilio Ficino and Giovanni Pico della Mirandola, both members of the brilliant circle of scholars, writers and artists associated with the Medici court in Florence in the 15th century, under the patronage of the great Cosimo de' Medici.

Marsilio Ficino (1433-99), a scholar, physician and priest, was commissioned by Cosimo to translate into Latin the Hermetic writings and the dialogues of Plato, together with the Neoplatonic writings of Porphyry, Proclus, Pseudo-Dionysus the Areopagite and Plotinus. The translation of the *Corpus Hermeticum* was ready in 1464 and published in 1471 under the title of *Pimander,* and the translations of Plato's dialogues, completed *c.* 1468, were published as the *Platonic Theology* in 1474.

Ficino's understanding, as that of others including St. Augustine, was that a divine theology or wisdom tradition, based on love, began simultaneously with Zoroaster among the Persians and with Hermes Trismegistus (*i.e.* Thoth) among the Egyptians. They believed that this wisdom tradition led in an unbroken chain to Plato via Orpheus and Pythagoras. It is this wisdom that is reputed to underlie the Hebrew, Orphic and Christian teachings, all of which developed from the blended Hermetic and Magian origin.

Demonstrating that this wisdom tradition was associated with Christianity, with links via Moses and the Zoroastrian Magi, Ficino was able to reconcile Platonic and Neo-Platonic philosophy with Christian theology. He regarded both philosophy and religion as being manifestations of a spiritual life, each needing the other in order to attain the *summum bonum* or greatest good.

According to the Neoplatonic philosophy that Ficino founded, love is the sustaining principle of the universe, and the attainment of the highest good is dependant not upon the Church but upon an impulse universal to man. The soul is not only immortal, but all souls by an inner urge naturally seek truth and goodness.

Ficino was immeasurably helped in the development of Neoplatonism by Giovanni Pico della Mirandola (1463-94). Pico joined Ficino's circle in 1484 and introduced Cabala into Ficino's Neoplatonism, being the founder or first great exponent of Christian Cabala. In this Pico was following in the footsteps of the poet-philosopher Ramon Lull, who in the 13th century, in Spain, brought together Jewish Cabala, Islamic mysticism and Christian revelation into a single method, which had an enormous influence on succeeding generations. As a result of Pico and Ficino's partnership, Neoplatonism became a universal philosophy, which blended Hebrew Cabala with the Hermetic, Neoplatonic and Christian teachings, making a synthesis of them all. As a result, the spiritual, magical and scientific core of Renaissance Neoplatonism was born.

Having travelled from Italy into France, this Renaissance Neoplatonism took a strong hold in England in the 16th century, beginning in King Henry VIII's time and reaching a zenith during the reign of Queen Elizabeth I, particularly in the works of William Shakespeare.

The Bible

Shakespeare's knowledge of the Bible is remarkably extensive and detailed. The teachings of the Bible pervade and underlie all his plays to such a degree that the plays seem, in fact, to be dramatised commentaries on and examples of the scriptural teachings, aided by Cabalistic philosophy and the Hermetic wisdom as well as by Shakespeare's extraordinary observation, insight into and knowledge of human nature.

Not for nothing then, it would seem, was an Englishman urged to possess a copy of both the Bible and the Shakespeare plays, and to always carry them with him when travelling.

The Teacher

Not only is Shakespeare a great poet, dramatist, Neoplatonic philosopher and Christian cabalist, but he is also a supreme teacher who teaches through entertainment, following the path of the ancients:

> The wisdom of the ancients devised a way of inducing men to study truth by means of pious frauds, the delicate Minerva secretly lurking beneath the mask of pleasure.[1]

Minerva is the Roman name for the Greek goddess of wisdom, Pallas Athena, the Tenth (and Chief) Muse, and the especial Muse of Shakespeare. Her Greek name literally means 'Spear Shaker', and she was renowned for shaking her spear of light at dark ignorance, exactly as Ben Jonson says of Shakespeare in his Folio tribute:

> For a good Poet's made, as well as borne.
> And such wert thou. Looke how the father's face
> > Lives in his issue, even so, the race
> Of Shakespeare's minde, and manners brightly shines
> > In his well torned, and true filed lines:
> In each of which, he seemes to shake a Lance,
> > As brandish't at the eyes of Ignorance.

The intention and hope of this series is to help reveal

Introduction

to lovers of Shakespeare some of the extraordinary and brilliant light concealed in Shakespeare's plays, and to pay homage to one who has been an exceptional friend and teacher to me and countless others—the great English Bard.

Foreword by Mark Rylance

The most striking characteristic of my friend Peter Dawkins is that he does in fact practise what he teaches others. The Philosophy he sees in *The Tempest* is a philosophy he lives by. You could say he walks his talk, especially as his other passion is Landscape and Architecture. He is a man equally concerned and knowledgeable about what is beneath his feet as above his head.

I find this particularly unusual amongst writers on Shakespeare, perhaps because most writers on Shakespeare don't imagine his work as philosophy, or as part of a philosophical movement in the Renaissance of Europe. We know so little about the actor from Stratford, and what we do know—the petty law suits against poachers for example—doesn't marry naturally with the deep compassion, wit and philosophical insight of the plays. But when we compare the plays with the teachings of the Greeks, Romans, Christians, and Jews, we find similar language and a similar search for good.

What do I mean by good? Well, I mean a similar search to distil accurate observation of human, natural and divine activity into a philosophy that helps people to be whole and realise their potential in life. Perhaps a simple way of expressing this is to compare us with England's patron, St. George, known as a warrior, but also, when he is not forced to fight the dragon, a gardener. All gardeners must learn when and how to plant, water and harvest their seed in order to survive. Well, as we learn more and more, both genetically and psychologically, about our soul's code, the seed of our soul, we should also turn to philosophy to learn how to grow those seeds. I mean by 'good' that it would be good for our souls to bear fruit in the actions of our lives.

I share Peter's belief that Shakespeare's work was intended by the author to help us create a garden for our souls. I believe he foresaw the growth of science, the division and politicising of religion, and also the decline of philosophy into an academic talking shop. He took a radical and inspired step, by applying the acute observation of natural science to human behaviour, freeing his work from any definite religious bias, and placing his observation, and the observation of the ancient philosophers, in the common and accessible world of popular entertainment, the theatre.

Since I met Peter eleven years ago, in 1989, he has helped me to understand why it is that everyone promotes Shakespeare as being so good for you. We know Shakespeare is entertaining, and his work a phenomenon amongst mankind's achievements, but what is he actually saying to us? There are many interpretations. I find Peter's one of the most beautiful and one that is beneficial to my life, enriching my ability to live intimately with myself, others, and the world around me, seen and unseen.

I first met Peter while playing *Hamlet* and *Romeo* at the Royal Shakespeare Company in Warwickshire. He lives in Warwickshire. Two friends had come to hear *Romeo* and began to speak about the alchemical imagery in the play. The use of lead, silver and gold to describe the interior states of *Romeo*. What they said made enormous sense to me. I asked them where they learnt this stuff, and they said why don't you come along tomorrow morning to this talk we're going to. So on Sunday morning, not a natural time for an actor playing Romeo and Hamlet to go anywhere, I dragged myself along to Peter's talk on *A Midsummer Night's Dream*.

He is a tall man, with a tall wife and even taller children. That Sunday I found myself entering a high ceilinged room, which he had built. He was an architect by profession. Thirty or so people were seated listening to him and a wild old gentleman, Sir George Trevelyan, speak about the meaning of *A Midsummer Night's Dream*. Peter is extremely humble, and

Foreword

speaks quietly. One has the curious impression that he is listening while he speaks. He is always thoroughly prepared with quotes and diagrams, some of which his sons illustrate for him. He never manages to get through them all, as the talk follows the intuition and enquiry of the group. His knowledge of Shakespeare and the Renaissance philosophical movements is astounding, yet he gets tremendously excited about discoveries, and breaks easily into fits of laughter when he gets things wrong. When I first met him, his shyness was tangible. Sir George, who had demanded many years before that Peter spoke about Shakespeare in front of people, would fall asleep after lunch next to Peter, wake with a start, and immediately fire off some of the best acting of Shakespeare I have had the privilege to hear. They were a right pair! But, my God, the love and enquiry into Shakespeare was deeper than I had ever encountered in any rehearsal room.

What I heard that day, and subsequently at the many talks of Peter's I have attended, changed my life as an actor, and inspired me with an appreciation of the foundations and architecture of the Shakespeare work.

That same year, my wife and I decided to begin to work directly with Peter on our productions of Shakespeare. *The Tempest* performed in the Rollright Stone Circle and subsequently at the site of Shakespeare's Globe, led me to meet Sam Wanamaker and later to become the first Artistic Director of the Globe in 1996. Both Sam and Sir George are sadly now gone. I hope that the spirit of their wonderful work lives on in the work that Peter and I do together.

I hope you enjoy this book. Try to remember Peter's laughter and doubt, if the written word doesn't answer your question or appears to have signed and sealed what continues to be an open enquiry.

Mark Rylance

Author's Preface

The Tempest, traditionally referred to as Shakespeare's last play, is reputedly the crown jewel of the Bard's dramatic works. With this I would whole-heartedly agree. Whether it is his best play in performance depends a lot on how and where it is produced, the actors' performances and the director's input; but when *The Tempest* is produced and acted well, it becomes sheer magic—which, of course, is what the play is about. Moreover, the play seems to summarise all that has gone before it and, more than any other Shakespeare play, provides an insight into the author and his Art, as well as into the knowledge and teachings of the Western Wisdom tradition. *The Tempest* has always fascinated me, and more than any other Shakespeare play has helped give me a gateway into the sometimes very secret world of our Western Wisdom.

Like the sacred scriptures and the Mysteries, the play has various levels of meaning and possible interpretation, which means that it can provide an almost endless source of knowledge and inspiration to whoever cares to look and feel beyond the first veil. Every time I read or experience a performance of it, for instance, I discover new things, and I am sure that this is, or can be, true for everyone. Moreover, each discovery can be inspirational or catalytic in one's life, providing explanations for the previously inexplicable and guidance as to the steps that might (or could) lie ahead.

This book is largely the result of various seminars that I gave in England during the summer of 1991, in tandem with the exciting open-air production of *The Tempest* performed by Mark Rylance and Claire Van Kampen's acting company, Phoebus Cart, with which I was involved as a friend and consultant. Having written it first as a much larger but unfinished volume, left to mature a while longer, I have drawn on those pages for this shorter, more condensed version for the Wisdom of Shakespeare series. What I have written in this book is by no means an attempt to make a consummate or infallible interpretation of this wonder play, as there are so many jewels of truth to be found in this treasure house of knowledge, but what I have written I hope that you will find useful.

The Tempest as a Mystery play has, of course, been written about before, as has its important psychological content and its Hermetic, Neoplatonic and Cabalistic background and sources, by such eminent scholars and authors as Colin Still, C. G. Jung, W. F. C. Wigston, Frances A. Yates, Noel Cobb, and some others less well known.[2] But there is a great deal more that could be said or is waiting to be discovered, and I share in this volume some fresh insights and discoveries that I have found over the course of many years of studying and enjoying the play. Not only this, but in these following pages I endeavour to show the direct association of the play and Shakespeare himself with the Rosicrucians and Freemasons of that vital 16th-17th century period in world history, and the ultimate importance of the play as a summary of the path of initiation.

For the plan of the book, I begin with a sketch of the play's background history, to set the scene in terms of the writing of the play. It was an exciting period in English history, during which the 'invisible' Brethren of the Rosie Cross were beginning to make their work known, and the first successful English colony was being established in North America. Both of those events influence the play profoundly, and the play can be seen as an integral part of those very events, especially the former.

The second chapter summarises the story of the play, scene by scene. This is not only for the benefit of those who

Preface

do not know the play very well, but also as a help to those who do, as it emphasises the key points that will be discussed in the book.

Since the play is essentially a Mystery play, based on ancient sources, the third chapter sets the scene in terms of the Ancient Mysteries, so that what Shakespeare is doing and what material he uses can be more easily seen.

After dealing with the background history, the story and the sources, the rest of the book (with the exception of the last chapter) devotes itself to peering into the play's profundity, discovering its light and its music. Its light is a profound wisdom concerning life and the human soul, whilst its music is to be found in the poetry, mathematics and rhythmical structures that underlie the outer sound of the spoken work.

Because Ariel is such a key figure in the play, the investigation begins with a chapter on this artful Spirit, to see what it really is or might be. After this comes a chapter (the fifth) identifying the major plots and themes. The sixth and seventh chapters deal with the major levels and stages of human evolution that are depicted in the play, together with our alchemical progression and initiation through these levels as allegorised in the stories of the characters.

The eighth chapter also deals with this allegorical portrayal of human evolution, but showing the 'planetary' progression of the story that is, as far as I know, unique to Shakespeare and Spenser, and which plays the seven 'notes' of Pan's pipes in a special creative sequence. Musicians interested in the harmony of the spheres and the underlying creative 'sound' of great poetry and drama should find this food for thought and further investigation.

The ninth chapter looks at the locations used in the play, which form a scenario analogous to the human body—a landscape temple, in other words, in which the Mystery is enacted. This is followed by a chapter devoted to the relationship and the meaning of the names of the characters, which helps to explain what they each represent in the context of the whole play; whilst the penultimate chapter (chapter eleven) discusses Prospero's Art—his magic.

The final chapter is on the Rosicrucians, of whom Prospero can be seen to be a personification. This chapter outlines a remarkable treasure trail of signposts and hints that link *The Tempest* and, indeed, the whole of the Shakespeare canon, to the Rosicrucians, and point to Shakespeare as being a Brother of the Rosie Cross.

As in the previous books of this series, I have used the Arden edition of *The Tempest* when quoting from the play, which I recommend both for its text and notes, although reference to a copy of the original Shakespeare folio is always worth the effort. Biblical quotes are from the Companion Bible. The works of Shakespeare and the Bible go together very well, and I recommend anyone who wishes to enjoy Shakespeare to the full, and understand the Bible more deeply, to have both on hand—as well as experiencing the play in performance, of course!

In this series I am not attempting to provide a bibliography as such, since this could be a weighty matter that unbalances the book itself; but the endnote references should provide ample scope for further research, and the treasure trail can be followed in this way, from one book or author to the next.

The material we are dealing with is Renaissance Neoplatonism, itself derived primarily from Christian, Hebraic, Neoplatonic and Platonic, Pythagorean, Orphic, Hermetic, Ancient Egyptian, Magian and Druidic sources. It is also Rosicrucian, and entirely relevant for this day and age. In exploring this material, and putting it into practice, I wish you great joy and the *freedom* that it eventually brings.

P.D. March 2000

1. Background

The *Tempest* was first printed in the 1st Folio of *Mr. William Shakespeares Comedies, Histories, & Tragedies,* published in 1623. The play is the first of the plays in the folio and occupies nineteen pages. It is listed as a Comedy, and heads the initial section of fourteen Comedies.

Written in 1610-11, *The Tempest* is now generally classed as one of Shakespeare's four great Romances which were produced between the years 1607-11 (*viz. Pericles,* 1607-8; *Cymbeline,* 1609-10; *The Winter's Tale,* 1610-11; *The Tempest,* 1610-11), and which form the peak (and culmination) of Shakespeare's art. Indeed, *The Tempest* is traditionally considered to be Shakespeare's last play, although this is held in doubt since *Henry VIII* appears to have been written later (*i.e.* possibly 1612-13). The answer may be that *The Tempest* was indeed the last Shakespeare drama to be written as a complete new play: *Henry VIII* (originally known as *All is True*) having been written earlier, in collaboration with John Fletcher, but revised and added to during 1612-13.[1]

The Tempest uses material not available until the latter part of 1610. Its first recorded performance took place before King James I at Whitehall on the night of Hallowmas, 1611, performed by Richard Burbage's company, the King's Men (formerly known as the Lord Chamberlain's Men and affectionately referred to nowadays as Shakespeare's Company). It was acted again before the Court during the Winter of 1612-13 by the King's Men, as part of the grand and prolonged entertainments provided for the visit of Frederick, the Elector Palatine, on his betrothal and subsequent marriage to King James' daughter, the Princess Elizabeth, on St Valentine's Day 1613.

Because of the masque scene conjured up for the young lovers by Prospero in *The Tempest,* and Prospero's emphasis on the importance of chastity before marriage, it has been suggested by several researchers that (a) this masque scene was inserted in 1612 specially for the betrothal celebrations, and (b) the performance took place before the royal couple on their betrothal night, 27th December 1612. If the dating is true, this has a double significance, since the 27th December is the annual festival of St John the Beloved (*i.e.* the Evangelist), the traditional feast day and annual assembly of the Rosicrucians and higher degree Freemasons.[2] The masque scene, however, must have been in the original version played in 1611 in order for the structure and meaning of the play to have been complete. This does not lessen its significance in any way as a perfect choice of play to be presented before the royal couple during the celebration of their betrothal.

The Tempest, deliberately placed as the first of the thirty-six plays in the 1623 Folio, and yet being the 'last' to be written, acts as a kind of foreword to the rest; for a good foreword is normally the last item to be written, is placed first in the book and summarises all that is to be found in a more detailed way in the rest of the publication. This *The Tempest* certainly does.

To all intents and purposes *The Tempest* is a pastoral drama concerned with the beneficial dominion of mankind over nature through virtue and art, in which the greatest art is the skilful knowledge and practice of love, or goodness. In this fashion it shares the basic themes of Edmund Spenser's *Faerie Queene*, in which seven of the attributes and virtues of King Arthur are personified and symbolically portrayed in a special order that is reiterated in *The Tempest*. But the dominant theme of *The Tempest* is founded upon Virgil's *Æneid*, in particular Book VI.

Book III of the *Æneid* concerns the visit of Æneas to the Isles of Shepherds, where the harpies snatch away the food. In Book VI, which provides the major basis of *The Tempest*, Virgil cryptically reveals the classical Mysteries of initiation, which allegorically led the candidate, *via* a tempest and the Underworld of Hades, through the Pillars of Hercules to the Fortunate Isles in the West. These magical Isles of Delight were equated with both the central sacred islands of Atlantis and also the 'apple-green' Avalon of King Arthur and Merlin, and this description from the Druidic and Arthurian Mysteries is also used in the play.

A large proportion of descriptive material for *The Tempest* is derived from the various accounts of the New Found Lands of America, which continent Dr. John Dee, Sir Francis Bacon and other Renaissance writers, sages and poets associated with the western mainland continent of Atlantis. For instance, Shakespeare's dramatic account of the tempest and Prospero's island is largely inspired by the report of the shipwreck of the *Sea-Adventure* upon the Bermuda Islands, which occurred on the 25 July 1609, and the subsequent experiences of the crew.

The *Sea-Adventure* story began in May 1609 when a fleet of nine ships and five hundred colonists on board set out from England to North America, to strengthen Captain John Smith's Virginian colony at Jamestown. This fleet was sponsored by the Virginia Company, whose principal shareholders and founding members of its Council included William, Earl of Montgomery and Philip, Earl of Pembroke (the 'Incomparable Paire' to whom the 1623 Shakespeare Folio is dedicated), the Earl of Salisbury, the Earl of Southampton, Sir Francis Bacon, Sir George Somers and Sir Thomas Gates.

Ever since the first three (failed) enterprises to colonise North America (in 1583, 1584 and 1587),[3] inspired largely by Dr. John Dee, the Sydney-Bacon-Essex group had worked on with the dream of establishing a new and enlightened society, a commonwealth, in a virgin land. The Newfoundland Company, founded in 1607, was one example of this group's enterprise, which began with a short-lived attempt to establish a fishing colony in Newfoundland, but then in 1610 succeeded in establishing Newfoundland as a colony.[4] The enterprise that first succeeded, however, was the Virginia one, named after Queen Elizabeth in whose reign the project had begun.

The Virginia Company was first formed as two separate Companies in 1606—the Virginia Company of London and the Virginia Company of Plymouth. Both sent ships to the New World, but only the London Virginia Company had early success, in the settling of Jamestown. The establishment of Jamestown, the first permanent English settlement in North America, took place on 14 May 1607 by an expedition consisting of three vessels—*Sarah Constant, Goodspeed* and *Discovery*—under the command of Captain John Smith. At Jamestown leadership was a problem, although Captain John Smith exerted some sort of control, and in 1609 the Company obtained a new royal charter establishing a new governing council composed entirely of company members who were empowered to appoint an all-powerful governor or governors in the colony. The new council decided on a single governor and appointed Sir Thomas West, Lord De la Warr, to the post. Sir Henry Hobart and Sir Francis Bacon, the

latter being at that time the King's Solicitor-General, prepared the charter for King James' signature. This charter of
1609 and the later one of 1612 were the beginnings of consti-
tutionalism in North America and the germ of the later
Constitution of the United States.

In the end Lord De la Warr was not able to leave England
and Sir Thomas Gates was appointed his substitute. Sir
Thomas Gates, together with Sir George Somers, sailed in the
flagship of the fleet, the *Sea-Adventure*. However, before the
fleet had reached the shores of America a storm blew up
which separated the *Sea-Adventure* from the rest of the fleet.
The wind drove the flagship towards the coast of the
Bermudas, where the crew were forced to run their ship
ashore. Before reaching the shore the ship 'fell in between
two rockes, where she was fast lodged and locked for further
budging'. All those on board managed to get safely to shore,
as well as saving a large part of the ship's fittings and stores.
The other ships of the fleet, with one exception, managed to
reach the mainland of America, with the belief that the *Sea-
Adventure* had perished with all aboard her. A report was sent
back to England before the end of 1609 giving news of the
storm and the supposed foundering of the *Sea-Adventure*.

The Bermudas had always been held in a mixture of awe
and fear by mariners, since those islands, uninhabited at that
time, appeared magical, with a constant stormy play of lightning and thunder around its great towering cliffs. No one
went near the islands if they could help it. Some thought
they were the abode of 'witches and devils, which grew by
reason of accustomed monstrous thunderstorms and tem-
pests'[5]; others that they were a remnant of the sacred islands
of Atlantis, ruled over by Poseidon (Neptune) and Zeus
(Jupiter).

The shipwrecked survivors discovered, however, that
the interior of the island upon which they were cast was like

a demi-paradise, fertile and with plenty of good food and water to sustain life. They continued to live there for a further nine months, managed to refloat and revictual the ship (which was preserved intact) and eventually sailed on to Virginia, reaching the Jamestown colony in May 1610.

The report of this 'miracle' arrived in England in the autumn of that year, together with some of the sailors involved. Various narratives of the wreck were published as a result. However, the official but confidential report on the Bermudas' shipwreck and on the state of Virginia generally was a private letter written by William Strachey, Sir Thomas Gates' secretary, to the Council members of the Virginia Company, entitled *The True Reportory of the Wracke and Redemption of Sir Thomas Gates*, dated 15 July 1610. This confidential report was not published until 1625, when it was included in *Purchas His Pilgrimes*,[6] but it is quite clear that Shakespeare was privy to it for he used details from the report in his play.

The Virginia Council, having received the report and heard other accounts from various survivors, published their own *True Declaration of the state of the Colonie in Virginia, with a confutation of such scandalous reports as have tended to the disgrace of so worthy an enterprise* (1610), in which were certain important moralisings that can be found as basic precepts in *The Tempest*, viz.:–

> What is there in all this Tragicall Comedie that should discourage us with impossibilitie of the enterprise? When of all the Fleete, one onely ship, by a secret leake was indangered and yet in the gulfe of Despair was so graciously preserved. *Quae videtur paena, est medicina*, that which we accompt a punishment against evill is but a medicine against evill.[7]
>
> *Omnis inordinatus animus sibi ipsi fit paena*, every inordinate soule becomes his own punishment.[8]

6

Background

Sylvester Jourdain's *Discovery of the Bermudas* (1610) also has comments relevant to *The Tempest*, viz.:–

> The Ilands of the Barmudas, as every man knoweth that hath heard or read of them, were never inhabited by any Christian or heathen people, but ever esteemed, and reputed, a most prodigious and inchanted place affoording nothing but gusts, stormes, and foule weather; and no man was ever heard, to make for the place, but as against their wils, they have…suffered shipwracke; yet did we find there the ayre so temperate and the Country so aboundantly fruitful of all fit necessaries, for the sustenation and preservation of man's life…[that we lived there comfortably for some nine months]. Wherefore my opinion is, that whereas it hath beene, and is still accounted, the most dangerous infortunate, and most forlorne place of the world, it is in truth the richest, healthfullest, and pleasing land…as ever man set foot upon.[9]

In William Strachey's report, *The True Reportory of the Wracke,* are the following relevant comments:–

> We found it to be the dangerous and dreaded Iland, or rather Ilands of the Bermuda. They be so terrible to all that ever touched on them, and such tempests, thunders, and other fearfull objects are seene and heard about them, that they be called commonly, The Devil's Ilands, and are feared and avoyded of all sea travellers alive, above any other place in the world. Yet it pleased our mercifull God, to make even this hideous and hated place, both the place of our safetie, and the meanes of our deliverance.

> And hereby also, I hope to deliver the world from a foule and generall errour: it being counted of most, that they can be no habitation for Men, but rather given over to Devils and wicked Spirits; whereas indeed wee find them now by experience, to bee as habitable and commodious as most Countries of the same climate and situation:

insomuch as if the entrance into them were as easie as the place it selfe is contenting, it had long ere this beene inhabited, as well as other Ilands. Thus shall we make it appeare, *That Truth is the daughter of Time, and that men ought not to deny every thing which is not subject to their owne sense.*[10]

Knowledge about the New World came from other sources too, and concerned not just Virginia and the Bermudas. Shakespeare was clearly most interested in the New World and well informed about it. Robert Eden's *History of Travaile* (1577), and Peter Martyr's *De Nouo Orbe,*[11] are worth mentioning: the former for the origin of the name *Setebos,* and the latter for such things as the supposed identification of the West Indies with Atlantis; the belief by the natives that the voyagers were gods descended from heaven; the native morality concerning possessions and stealing (*i.e.* knowing no difference between 'mine' and 'thine'); the 'horrible roarings of the wild beastes in the woodes'; the repugnant bats compared to 'ravenous harpies'; the custom of the Spanish conquistadors to hunt the natives with dogs; the observation that the natives 'were wonderfully astonied at the sweete harmony' of music; the native dancing; the 'certayne wild men...without any certaine language'; certain numbers of Indians who, after being cared for and educated as Christians, became the treacherous enemies of 'the Monastery where they had been brought up with fatherly charity'; the countryside abounding in 'wild Boares, thorny Hedghogges, and Porkepennes'; attacks by wild apes; and a 'Monster of the Sea like a Man'. Some of these and other matters concerning the New World were also reported elsewhere, such as the strange 'burthen' ('*bowgh wawgh*') of Ariel's first song, recorded in James Rosier's account of a ceremonial Virginian dance, published in *Purchas His Pilgrimage* (1613).[12] Shakespeare also probably knew Sir Walter Raleigh, or at least the accounts of Raleigh's voyages.[13]

Background

Other source material is gathered from Ovid's
Metamorphoses and Michel Montaigne's essay, *Of the Canibales.*
Furthermore, *The Tempest* shares many of the plot features to
be found in the *scenari* of the popular sixteenth century Italian
pastoral tragi-comedy, known as *Commedia dell'Arte,* which
was in vogue at the Courts of mainland Europe, particularly
in the French Court of the Valois kings, and which had visited
England in the 16th century prior to 1578.

Besides Chaucer, who was an important source of inspiration and material for both Spenser and Shakespeare, certain definite Pythagorean, Platonic, Hermetic and Cabalistic
influences on Shakespeare's philosophy and its presentation
in his drama, of which *The Tempest* would appear to be the
grand finale and summary, should also be mentioned: such
as Plotinus' *Enneads* (edited by Porphyry), Roger Bacon's
Book of the Six Sciences, Opus Maius and other writings,
Raymond Lull's *Tractatus de Astronomia* (1297), Marsilio
Ficino's *Theologia Platonica* (1474), *De Triplici Vita* and *De Vita
Coelitus Comparanda,* Pico della Mirandola's *Conclusions* (1486)
and *Apology* (1487), Johann Reuchlin's *De Verbo Mirifico* (1494)
and *De Arte Cabbalistica* (1517), Francesco Giorgi's *De
Harmonia Mundi* (1525) and *In Scripturum Sacram Problemata*
(1536), Henry Cornelius Agrippa's *De Incertitudine et Vanitate
Scientiarum et Artium* (1531) and *De Occulta Philosophia* (1533),
Geronimo Cardano's *On Subtlety* (1552) and *On the Variety of
Things* (1556). Indeed, *The Tempest*, like the rest of the
Shakespeare works, belongs firmly to the Neoplatonic,
Hermetic and Christian-Cabalist movement or occult tradi-
tion of the Renaissance. (I recommend the scholarly works of
Frances Yates and Manly Palmer Hall for a fuller discussion of
this vitally important line of influence upon Shakespeare.)[14]

In addition to the above there is all the source material
for Neoplatonism, such as the works by Pythagoras, Plato
and Aristotle, which themselves are developed from the

works of earlier philosophers and the mystical rites, teachings and hymns of Orpheus; all of which were transformed into Neoplatonism and then Christian Neoplatonism, and finally Renaissance Christian Neoplatonism.

Included in this list and line of influence must be placed Dr. John Dee, an Elizabethan magus of repute and a contemporary of Shakespeare, of whose character something is personified in the character of Prospero. Dee was particularly renowned for his cryptography, occult mathematics and cabalistic experiments in angel conjuring, although this was by no means his only field of study and experimentation. At one time he possessed England's largest and most comprehensive library of books, which he allowed his scientific and scholarly friends to use. The major part of this library was on the subjects of poetry, drama, architecture and occult (or cabalistic) mathematics, whilst its core was composed of an almost complete collection of *prisci theologia*,[15] which included the *Corpus Hermeticum*.

Dee's *Preface* to the first published English translation of *Euclides Elementes* (1570), his *Monas Hieroglyphica* (1564) and his *General and Rare Memorials pertayning to the Perfecte Arte of Navigation* (1577), with their Freemasonic and Rosicrucian tone, had a profound influence both in England and in Europe.[16] Moreover, Dee was a moving spirit behind both the colonisation of the New World and the revival of the Arthurian Golden Age. The Elizabethan Age, including Shakespeare, owed a great debt to Dee. Yet Dee seems to have made a serious mistake by falling into bad company, using the mediumistic (and possible charlatan) Kelly for his supposed angel contacts; so that when Dee returned from his continental mission in 1589 he had fallen from Elizabeth's royal favour, then was repudiated and disgraced in the reign of James I by the superstitious king, and died in abject poverty in 1608.

Background

The name of Ariel as a spirit or angel was certainly not unknown in Shakespeare's time. It occurs in Hebraic and Christian cabalistic tradition, and is mentioned in the *Steganographia* of Trithemius, wherein Ariel is listed as one of the twenty-eight planetary angels. Dee must have known about Ariel, and Shakespeare's knowledge concerning this great spirit is profounder than it appears at first sight. Ariel is the name of a great archangel known to the various secret societies in Europe who studied and practised cabalistic magic, as well as being a word-play upon the Neoplatonist's 'Airy' realm of the angels. It is worth noting that a contemporary Frenchman, Président de Thou, recorded that a gentleman called Beaumont was tried and found guilty of magical practices by a court at Angoulême in 1596. Two years after, at a conference at which de Thou was present (and no torture was in prospect), Beaumont had freely confessed that he himself

> ...held a commerce with Aërial and Heavenly Spirites... That Schools and Professors of this noble Art, had been frequent in all Parts of the World, and still were so in Spain, at Toledo, Cardona, Grenada and other Places: That they had also been formerly celebrated in Germany, but for the most part had failed, ever since Luther had sown the Seeds of his Heresy, and began to have so many Followers: that in France and in England it was still secretly preserved, as it were by Tradition, in the Families of certain Gentlemen; but that only the initiated were admitted into the Sacred Rites; to the exclusion of profane Persons...[17]

The reference to the magical Art, which is undoubtedly the Christian-Neoplatonic Hermetic-Cabalistic Art, being preserved as a tradition in the families of certain gentlemen in England and France is most revealing. It would seem that Dee and Shakespeare were amongst them.

Until his library was burnt by a mob, Dee at one time possessed the best collection ever made of manuscripts and books by Roger Bacon, the 13th century Franciscan friar and the first known Englishman to cultivate alchemical philosophy. Roger Bacon was a great and illumined magus, who was reputed to have had the ability to conjure angels and work miracles, although he had to be very circumspect and secret about such matters, and as a result employed cryptographic methods widely. He was honoured with the title of 'Doctor Mirabilis'. Perhaps even more than John Dee, Roger Bacon seems to have been a part model for the character of Prospero.

In addition, the close association of thought between Francis Bacon's philosophical works and the Shakespeare dramatic works should be noted—Francis Bacon being another Elizabethan/Jacobean magus of the Christian-Neoplatonic Hermetic-Cabalistic tradition, but a more careful, secret and successful one than Dee. Francis Bacon, to all intents and purposes, seems to have deliberately carried on the work begun by his predecessor and namesake, Roger Bacon, handed on to him by Dee and others, and was in his own right a great philosopher-poet, cryptographist and teacher, who was compared to Plato by his contemporaries[18] and named as a 'Second Apollo', 'Chancellor of Parnassus', 'the Tenth Muse' and 'Leader of the Choir of Muses',[19] who, as a 'concealed poet',[20] renovated Philosophy 'walking humbly in the socks of Comedy' and 'After that, more elaborately he rises on the loftier buskin of Tragedy…'.[21]

The Tempest actually appears to be a dramatised portrayal of Bacon's scheme for the advancement and proficience of learning; especially what he terms the 'Active Science'.[22] In this *active* science human beings would, like Prospero, be able to command the very elements of nature, through a practical knowledge of the laws of nature, physical and metaphysical, but with everything dedicated to doing good—*i.e.* to charity or mercy. Prospero, therefore, can be seen as a prototype of the Rosicrucian philosopher-scientists illustrated in Bacon's utopian story, the *New Atlantis*, as the brethren of Salomon's House or College of the Six Days' Work. The first version of *The Advancement and Proficience of Learning* had been published in 1605, but the fuller version, translated into Latin as the *De Augmentis Scientiarum*, was not published until 1623. The *New Atlantis* was published in 1626/7.

One other fascinating source is the *History of Ludovic Sforza, Duke of Milan*, particularly because of its link with Boccalini's *Ragguagli di Parnasso*, of which the 77th Advertisement, *The Universal and General Reformation of the Whole Wide World*, was used to introduce the *Fama Fraternitatis* of the Rosicrucians. The *General Reformation* and *Fama* were first published in August 1614 but were circulating in manuscript at the time that *The Tempest* was written.

The Palatinate Court at Heidelberg of the Elector Frederick and Princess Elizabeth became a major focus of Rosicrucian thought and development in Germany, and it is significant that *The Tempest* was acted before them immediately prior to their marriage and departure for Germany. On this Frances Yates comments acutely:-

> Shakespeare gave them the blessing of his Rosicrucian manifesto; Prospero represents the Elizabethan occult philosophy, revived, and about to be exported as Rosicrucianism.[23]

This Rosicrucian association is given further weight by Ben Jonson's masque, *The Fortunate Isles and their Union*, designed for the Court on the Twelfth Night, 1626. This Jonsonian masque is a parody of *The Tempest* and a cryptic satire on the Rosicrucians. In itself it is not source material for *The Tempest*, as it was written later, but it alludes to certain

Rosicrucian matters and influences which are embodied in *The Tempest*, whilst at the same time providing indications of the esoteric meanings of various characters and events in Shakespeare's play.

Ben Jonson was involved in the publication of the 1623 Shakespeare Folio, contributing the longest and most beautiful of the four tributes to Shakespeare that preface the Folio after Heminge's and Condell's Dedication and Foreword. This is the encomium that refers to Shakespeare as 'my beloved' and as seeming 'to shake a Lance, as brandish't at the eyes of Ignorance'. Jonson had published a folio of his own works just a few years previously, and his experience both in that publication as well as in play writing was probably most valuable. He may have been helpful in other ways too. From the evidence of his various masques and plays, Jonson was certainly privy to many matters concerning Shakespeare that were concealed from the general public behind a veil of mystery. His role in these matters may possibly be hinted at in a 1645 adapted version of the first Rosicrucian manifesto, wherein Jonson is alluded to as the 'Keeper of the Trophonian Denne'.[24]

The Trophonian Den refers to the deep cave of Trophonius, who with his brother was the architect of the Temple of Apollo at Delphi. The Delphic temple was built over the sacred fissure in the Parnassian rock (called 'the well of Cassotis'), where the Pythia or mediumistic priestess delivered the oracle. The Trophonian cave is described as being near Lebadea in Boetia, where the spirit of Trophonius was the oracle. In order to undergo initiation into the mysteries of life and achieve the wisdom, illumination and blessings of Paradise, the dark cavern had to be entered alone. This could only be done when preceded and accompanied by rigorous fasts, ablutions and other rites. It was said that those who entered the cave to hear the oracle returned again with serious faces and a melancholy disposition. Interestingly, Prospero is the 'Oracle' in *The Tempest* who rectifies the lords' knowledge (v, i, 243).

Not only does the Trophonian association with Apollo, Parnassus and the Delphic oracle provide a direct allegorical connection with the Rosicrucians and their *Fama Fraternitatis,* but in addition the story of *The Tempest,* largely based upon Virgil's account of Æneas and his descent into the underground world at Cumæ near Naples, has a direct parallel to the story of the Trophonian Den. It should also be noted that the signature of Ben Jonson on his famous memorial verse to Shakespeare, printed at the front of the 1623 Folio, is in the form of his two initials, *B. J.*, which just happen to be the initials of the two great pillars (*Boaz* and *Jachin*) which stood at the gateway to the temple of Solomon, as is well-known to Freemasons and Cabalists everywhere.

Likewise it should be mentioned, as it certainly seems to me to be not by chance, that Ben Jonson also produced a play about a magician and the occult sciences. It was called *The Alchemist* and was performed in 1610 by the King's Men (*i.e.* Shakespeare's Company). Its first printing was in 1612. As in his *Fortunate Isles,* in *The Alchemist* Jonson goes out of his way to satirise not only magic and magicians but also (seemingly) the whole early-17th century Hermetic-Scientific and Neoplatonic-Cabalistic movement (*i.e.* the Rosicrucians), which in this instance he does by sketching a portrait of a charlatan magician who, in the company of a whore, deliberately cheats society. *The Alchemist* even parodies the masque scene in *The Tempest* with a fake vision of the Fairy Queen presented by the false magician to one of his weak-minded dupes.

But, despite his satire, Jonson was also a proven supporter of the Arthurian and Elizabethan 'Fairie' revival that is based upon the very movement he appears to satirise. He not only appears to pour scorn on Shakespeare in some instances, but in another breath he adulates the great author. Moreover, Jonson was deeply involved with the publication of the 1623 Shakespeare Folio. Seeing that it is a well-known fact that light shows up best when contrasted with the dark, or the serious with the ridiculous, perhaps Ben Jonson was deliberately employed by those 'in the know' to provide such contrast and interest?

The complete and perfect polarity to Shakespeare's *Tempest* is Marlowe's *Dr. Faustus,* first performed in 1594, published in 1604, and republished with major additions and reworking in 1616. *Dr. Faustus* appeared at the beginning of the Shakespeare story—*Venus and Adonis* having being published in March 1593 as the 'first heir' of Shakespeare's invention and the first work to have the name of Shakespeare printed on it.

Dr. Faustus is about a famed and learned man who, unlike Prospero in *The Tempest,* chooses to ally himself with the forces and demons of Evil. He does this for the sake of acquiring all-knowledge, but for entirely selfish reasons. In complete contrast to the story of *The Tempest,* Faustus continually rejects the proffered hand of mercy from the good angel right to the bitter end, by which time it is too late. His life becomes utterly degenerate, wasted and emptied of anything worthwhile. The knowledge he acquires becomes increasingly petty and sordid, his visions and behaviour grow more and more debased, and the play ends with Faustus being claimed by the jaws of hell.

The Tempest, on the other hand, shows the exact opposite, depicting a famed and learned man who chooses to ally himself with the forces and spirit of Good, who dedicates himself to virtue and the acquisition of knowledge beneficial to all, who cares for others and, in particular, his own child whom he calls his 'heart'. (Faustus, by contrast, is loveless and childless.) Prospero's mind soars into the heavens: he perceives the spirits or angels of God and is able to commune with and even command them. He does good to others; and he eventually enters the very heart of the divine mystery of love, with mercy being given by him unconditionally to all. In other words he sets love, the true Master, free.

As with the Jonson plays, it would almost seem as if the Marlowe-Shakespeare plays formed some kind of conspiracy, as part of a great plan—*Dr. Faustus* being presented at the beginning and *The Tempest* at the end of the Shakespeare cycle; the first being a study in the possible ultimate fall of man, and the last being a study in the possible ultimate resurrection of man. This Marlowe-Shakespearean sequence follows a similar order as that of the Mysteries: first, the descent into the Underworld of Hades, followed by an ascent into an 'island' of comedies and tragedies, completed by the final ascent to the palace and dwelling-place of Light.

It is rather fascinating that the time period of eighteen years from 1593–1611 is associated with a Rosicrucian signature, surviving in modern Freemasonry as the unique 18th Degree, Knight of the Rose Cross, and that 'Shake-speare' is a cryptonym for a Rosicrucian, whose role as a 'St George' figure is to shake his lance of love-light at the dragon of vice and ignorance in order to transform the dragon into a dove.

> …*Looke how the father's face*
>   *Lives in his issue, even so, the race*
> *Of* Shakespeares *minde, and manners brightly shines*
>   *In his well torned, and true filed lines:*
> *In each of which, he seemes to shake a Lance,*
>   *As brandish'd at the eyes of ignorance.*[25]

17

THE TEMPEST.

Actus primus, Scena prima.

A tempestuous noise of Thunder and Lightning heard: Enter a Ship-master, and a Botesvvaine.

Master.

Ote-swaine.

Botef. Heere Master: What cheere?

Mast. Good: Speake to th'Mariners: fall too't, yarely, or we run our selues a ground, bestirre, bestirre. *Exit.*

Enter Mariners.

Botef. Heigh my hearts, cheerely, cheerely my harts: yare, yare: Take in the toppe-sale: Tend to th'Masters whistle: Blow till thou burst thy winde, if roome enough.

Enter Alonso, Sebastian, Anthonio, Ferdinando, Gonzalo, and others.

Alon. Good Botefwaine haue care: where's the Master? Play the men.

Botef. I pray now keepe below.

Anth. Where is the Master, Boson?

Botef. Do you not heare him? you marre our labour, Keepe your Cabines: you do assist the storme.

Gonz. Nay, good be patient.

Botef. When the Sea is: hence, what cares these roarers for the name of King? to Cabine; silence: trouble vs not.

Gon. Good, yet remember whom thou hast aboord.

Botef. None that I more loue then my selfe. You are a Counsellor, if you can command these Elements to silence, and worke the peace of the present, wee will not hand a rope more, vse your authoritie: If you cannot, giue thankes you haue liu'd so long, and make your selfe readie in your Cabine for the mischance of the houre, if it so hap. Cheerely good hearts: out of our way I say. *Exit.*

Gon. I haue great comfort from this fellow: methinks he hath no drowning marke vpon him, his complexion is perfect Gallowes: stand fast good Fate to his hanging, make the rope of his destiny our cable, for our owne doth little aduantage: If he be not borne to bee hang'd, our case is miserable. *Exit.*

Enter Botefwaine.

Botef. Downe with the top-Mast: yare, lower, lower, bring her to Try with Maine-course. A plague——

A cry within. Enter Sebastian, Anthonio & Gonzalo.

upon this howling: they are lowder then the weather, or our office: yet againe? What do you heere? Shal we giue ore and drowne, haue you a minde to sinke?

Sebas. A poxe o'your throat, you bawling, blasphemous incharitable Dog.

Botef. Worke you then.

Anth. Hang cur, hang, you whorefon insolent Noyse-maker, we are lesse afraid to be drownde, then thou art.

Gonz. I'le warrant him for drowning, though the Ship were no stronger then a Nutt-shell, and as leaky as an vnstanched wench.

Botef. Lay her a hold, a hold, set her two courses off to Sea againe, lay her off.

Enter Mariners wet.

Mari. All lost, to prayers, to prayers, all lost.

Botef. What must our mouthes be cold?

Gonz. The King, and Prince, at prayers, let's assist them, for our case is as theirs.

Sebas. I'am out of patience.

An. We are meerly cheated of our liues by drunkards, This wide-chopt-rascall, would thou mightst lye drowning the washing of ten Tides.

Gonz. Hee'l be hang'd yet,
Though euery drop of water sweare against it,
And gape at widst to glut him. *A confused noyse within.*
Mercy on vs.
We split, we split, Farewell my wife, and children,
Farewell brother: we split, we split, we split.

Anth. Let's all sinke with' King

Seb. Let's take leaue of him. *Exit.*

Gonz. Now would I giue a thousand furlongs of Sea, for an Acre of barren ground: Long heath, Browne firrs, any thing; the wills aboue be done, but I would faine dye a dry death. *Exit.*

Scena Secunda.

Enter Prospero and Miranda.

Mira. If by your Art (my deerest father) you haue Put the wild waters in this Rore, alay them:
The skye it seemes would powre down stinking pitch, But that the Sea, mounting to th' welkins cheeke, Dashes the fire out. Oh! I haue suffered With those that I saw suffer: A braue vessell
(Who

A

1. THE TEMPEST, SHAKESPEARE FOLIO (1623)

The page is headed by the 'Blind Boy' headpiece, sometimes known as the 'Cupid', 'Dionysus' or 'Archer' headpiece.

2. LAST PAGE, THE TEMPEST, SHAKESPEARE FOLIO (1623)

2. The Story

Act 1, Scene 1—On a ship at sea

A ship carrying King Alonso of Naples, his brother Sebastian and his son Ferdinand, together with Duke Antonio of Milan, Gonzalo, councillor to the king, and two lords, Adrian and Francisco, plus their retinue of servants, is caught in a storm. The master and boatswain give orders to their men, and the boatswain attempts to keep the lords below deck, out of the way. The ship hits rocks and all the passengers, terrified, jump overboard.

Act 1, Scene 2—On an island, before Prospero's cell.

Miranda, the daughter of Prospero, suspects that her father has created the storm by using his magical art. She witnessed the shipwreck and pleads with her father to allay the storm, her heart weeping for the poor souls on the ship. Prospero calms her and assures her that there is no harm done, and that he has done nothing but in care of her, his only daughter. He then proceeds to inform Miranda of their past history, the time having come to do so.

Prospero explains that he was once the Duke of Milan, but that he was deposed by his younger brother, Antonio, whom he trusted to manage his estate. This was a weakness on his part, for he preferred to study the liberal arts and sciences than to govern his land and people. It awakened an evil nature in his brother, who then took advantage of the situation. To achieve his aim Antonio made a contract with King Alonso of Naples, an enemy to Prospero, to give the king homage and tribute if he should make him, Antonio, duke of Milan once Prospero and his issue were done away with.

Miranda was not quite three years old when the deposition took place. Having assembled an army secretly, at midnight on the chosen day the conspirators forcibly hurried Prospero and his daughter away from the city. Not daring to murder them on land, the conspirators took their captives aboard a bark and sailed out to sea for some leagues, where they put the duke and his two-year old daughter in a small rotten boat, without mast or sail, and cast them adrift. However, the kindly councillor, Gonzalo, who had been put in charge of this scheme, had managed to store aboard many supplies for the castaways, including fine linen and clothes, food, water, and Prospero's prized books. By divine providence they arrived at an island where they were able to land, where they have lived ever since.

Prospero then reveals that an auspicious moment has arrived, marked by a star, bringing an opportunity that he must not miss. He magically puts Miranda to sleep and calls Ariel, a spirit who serves him. Ariel reports that he has performed all that was asked of him by Prospero—that he raised the tempest, caused the ship to become locked in a deep nook between rocks, appeared like fire on the vessel so as to frighten the passengers into quitting it, and then made sure that they came safely to land, unharmed. The mariners he has left safely asleep below deck in the ship, the lords and their servants he has dispersed about the island, and the rest of the fleet he has sent sailing home to Milan believing that the king's ship was wrecked and the king had perished.

Prospero thanks Ariel, and Ariel asks for his liberty in return for his services. Prospero refuses this, as the time is not yet 'out' for this to happen, and reminds Ariel of how he, Prospero, released him from magical imprisonment in the cleft trunk of a pine tree, having been put there by the now-dead witch, Sycorax, when Ariel would not obey her foul commands. Ariel apologises, and Prospero promises Ariel his freedom after two days if Ariel will continue to carry out his commands.

Having sent Ariel away on another errand, requiring him to be invisible to all except himself, Prospero wakes Miranda, his 'dear heart'. They go to visit their slave, Caliban, the dead witch's half-human son, to order him to fetch more fuel for the fire. Caliban complains of his slavery, but Prospero retorts that he has justly deserved it, having tried to rape Miranda after he had been taken in, cared for and educated by Prospero.

Ariel then returns, invisibly leading Ferdinand, who follows the sound of music created by Ariel. Ferdinand is sorrowful, believing his father drowned, but Ariel's song gives him comfort. Miranda, when she sees Ferdinand arriving, is amazed and delighted, he being the first young man she has seen—and the only man other than her father and Caliban. Ferdinand is equally enchanted, and Prospero observes, much to his own delight and according to his plans, that they have immediately fallen in love with each other. However, to ensure that they do not take their love too lightly, especially Ferdinand, he pretends to distrust the prince and, despite Miranda's pleas, magically overpowers the young man and manacles his neck and feet together, as a prisoner.

Act 2, Scene 1—Another part of the island

The lords are all gathered together on another part of the island. King Alonso is fraught with sorrow at the supposed loss of his son and heir, and Gonzalo, the good old councillor, tries to cheer him up. Despite the satirical remarks of Antonio and Sebastian, Gonzalo and Adrian point out that the island is actually very pleasant and green, that they are fortunate in being alive, and that their garments, despite being drenched in the sea, seem fresh and new-dyed as when they first put them on at the marriage of Alonso's daughter Claribel to the King of Tunis. After quibbling about the story of Queen Dido and whether Tunis was Carthage, Francisco tells the king that he saw Ferdinand swimming bravely towards land and that he doubted not that the king's son was alive. Alonso, however, will not be cheered up. Sebastian tells his brother, the king, that he (Alonso) is to blame for the loss of his son because he married his daughter, against her will and that of all the others, to an African instead of to a European.

Trying to lift the mood again, Gonzalo muses on what he would do if he were king of the island, describing his kind of utopia to the others. Whilst he is doing this, and Antonio and Sebastian mock him, Ariel arrives (invisible), playing solemn music. This makes all the royal party fall asleep except Sebastian and Antonio, who then, at Antonio's suggestion, plot to take this opportunity to kill Alonso and make Sebastian king. However Prospero, by his art, has seen the danger; so, as the would-be murderers draw their swords, Ariel returns and sings in Gonzalo's ear about the conspiracy, awakening him to possible danger. Gonzalo in turn awakens the king, who enquires why Sebastian and Antonio have their swords drawn. They reply that it is because they heard a terrible bellowing, maybe of bulls or lions. They all decide to move on and seek the king's son.

Act 2, Scene 2—Another part of the island

Caliban is gathering wood for the fire, to the sound of thunder, when Trinculo, a jester, appears on the scene. Caliban is frightened at the appearance of Trinculo, thinking him a spirit come to torment him, so he falls flat on the ground hoping not to be disturbed. Trinculo, looking for shelter from the threatening storm, discovers Caliban and wonders what he is—whether man or fish, dead or alive. A thunderclap makes him seek shelter under Caliban's cloak.

Stephano, a butler, arrives, bottle in hand and drunk. He thinks the cloak, which is moving and muttering strange sounds, is a strange two-headed, four-legged monster. Hoping to tame the monster and exhibit him for money, he feeds Caliban with some wine from his bottle; but Trinculo calls out, recognising the voice of Stephano. The two friends are joyfully reunited. Caliban, who is delighted with his first taste of wine, thinks that Stephano must be a god and vows to serve him instead of Prospero from now on. He leads the two servants towards a place where food can be found, singing drunkenly and proclaiming 'high-day, freedom!'

Act 3, Scene 1—Before Prospero's cell

Ferdinand, at Prospero's command, is engaged in piling up logs before the cell. He finds that his labours are made sweet by the sympathy he receives from Miranda. Miranda wants to help so that he can rest, but Ferdinand will not hear of it. Prospero, looking on secretly, sees that Miranda has completely fallen in love with Ferdinand, whilst Ferdinand in turn is captivated by her. They confess their love for each other and make a troth to marry. Prospero, still concealed from them, is delighted and prays that their love may be blessed.

Act 3, Scene 2—Another part of the island

Caliban, Trinculo and Stephano are drunk. Caliban complains to Stephano and Trinculo that he is subject to a tyrant and sorcerer (Prospero), who has cheated him of his island. He asks that they help him take revenge by murdering Prospero, by first seizing his books to take away his magic power, and then knocking a nail into his head, or braining him with a log, or disembowelling him with a stake, or cutting his throat with a knife. He suggests that Stephano could then be lord of the island and Caliban his servant, and that Stephano should then possess the beautiful Miranda and have heirs by her. Stephano and Trinculo agree to this proposition and they shake hands on it, meaning to carry out the deed whilst Prospero is asleep. They try to sing, but Ariel, who has watched them, plays the tune on his tabor and pipe, which alarms the two castaways. Caliban tells them not to be frightened and explains that the island is full of noises, sounds and sweet airs that give delight and hurt not. Encouraged, they determine to follow the sound, and thereby Ariel leads them away.

Act 3, Scene 3—Another part of the island

The lords have wandered around the island as if in a maze. Gonzalo declares he can go no further. Alonso decides that they will never find his son, who must be drowned, and that they must let him go. Antonio and Sebastian have not given up their plan to murder Alonso and Gonzalo, and plot to carry out the deed that night, when the others are weary with their travel and cannot be so watchful.

At that moment they hear strange solemn music. Invisibly overseen by Prospero, a banquet is magically brought before the men by strange 'shapes' that dance about it and invite the king and his company to eat. Astonished, Alonso and Gonzalo remark upon the sweet and harmonious music, whilst Sebastian declares that now he will believe that there are unicorns, and that in Arabia there is one tree, the phoenix throne, with one phoenix at that hour reigning there. Antonio also expresses belief in such fables. Encouraged by Gonzalo, they step forward to eat, even though it might be their last meal.

Suddenly, to the sound of thunder and flash of lightning, Ariel appears in the form of a harpy. Clapping his wings, he makes the banquet disappear. He addresses Alonso, Sebastian and Antonio, admonishing them as three men of sin, unfit to live, who have been flung by destiny upon the island. He causes them to be mad, suggesting that even with such-like valour men hang and drown their proper selves. The lords draw their swords, thinking to defend themselves, but are mocked by Ariel, who declares that he and his spirit fellows are ministers of Fate and, like the wind, invulnerable. Ariel reminds them how they supplanted Prospero and cast him and his child to sea, to die, and how now the seas and shores and all the creatures are incensed by the powers against their peace. He declares to Alonso how the powers have, as a result, bereft him of his son, and that they do pronounce by him (Ariel) a sentence of lingering perdition—one of heart-sorrow but with a clear life ensuing.

Overwhelmed with sorrow and guilt, Alonso heads towards the sea to drown himself, followed by Sebastian and Antonio who madly attempt to fight the spirits with their swords. Gonzalo beseeches the other lords to follow after them, to prevent the three men of sin from causing harm to themselves.

Act 4, Scene 1—Before Prospero's cell.

Prospero has freed Ferdinand and apologises to him for the austere punishment that, he explains, was but to test Ferdinand's strength of love for his daughter. Agreeing to their marriage, Prospero declares that he is giving away one third of his life, or that for which he lives. He urges Ferdinand not to take Miranda's virginity before the wedding ceremony. Calling Ariel and thanking him and Ariel's spirit helpers for performing their tasks so well, Prospero asks Ariel to bring the 'rabble' (spirit actors) so as to perform a 'trick', a masque for the young couple, as they expect it of him.

At Prospero's command Ariel returns with many spirits to act the parts required. The magical pageant unfolds as Miranda and Ferdinand watch, entranced. The mystical form of the goddess Iris appears first, then Juno, then Ceres, to celebrate the contract of love and give a blessing on the young lovers. This is followed by the appearance of nymphs and then reapers, to help celebrate the love-bond. With the appearance of the reapers Prospero starts. He is reminded of the foul conspiracy against his life, the time for their plot to be fulfilled having almost come. He dismisses the spirits and explains to Ferdinand that the actors were all spirits, melted now into thin air, and that he and all creatures are similarly made of such stuff as dreams, and that their lives are all rounded with a sleep. He urges them to retire into his cell whilst he takes a walk to still his vexed and beating mind.

Once alone, Prospero calls Ariel 'with a thought'. He tells Ariel that they must prepare to meet with Caliban. Ariel explains that he has left the 'varlets' in a filthy scum-covered pool. To prepare for their coming to the cell, Prospero tells Ariel to hang up his fine 'glistering apparel' on a line before the cell. When Caliban, Trinculo and Stephano approach the cell, the butler and jester are indeed attracted by the clothing and want to put it on. Caliban tries to tell them that it is trash and that they should not forget their purpose, but to no avail. The two drunk and murderous friends fight over who should wear the best costumes, and laden Caliban with as many garments to carry as they can.

Various spirits in the shape of dogs and hounds enter, set on by Prospero and Ariel, and Caliban, Trinculo and Stephano are driven away. Prospero then declares that all his enemies now lie at his mercy, and that shortly all his labours shall end and Ariel shall have his freedom.

Act 5, Scene 1—Before Prospero's cell.

Ariel and Prospero, in his magic robes, talk together. Ariel reveals that he has left the king and his followers in the lime grove that protects Prospero's cell from the weather, where they cannot budge until Prospero releases them. He recounts to Prospero how the king, his brother and Prospero's brother are all distracted, with the others mourning over them, 'brimful of sorrow and dismay'—especially 'the good old lord, Gonzalo', whose tears run down his beard. Appealing to the compassionate side of Prospero's nature, Ariel declares that if Prospero could now behold them, his affections would become tender. Questioned further by Prospero, Ariel remarks that his own affections would become tender if he were human. At this, Prospero declares that his affections, being human, certainly will become so, and that the rarer action is in virtue rather than in vengeance. Since the three men of sin have become penitent, his purpose is complete. He sends Ariel to release them and bring them to him.

Whilst Ariel is gone on this mission, Prospero ritually renounces his 'potent Art', his 'rough magic', calling upon some heavenly music to work his end, breaking his magic staff and burying it deep in the earth, and drowning his book of magic.

When Ariel returns with the king and his party, Prospero conducts them into the magic circle that he has made, where they stand charmed. Prospero speaks to them, forgiving Alonso, Sebastian and Antonio for their sins against him, and Sebastian and Antonio for their sin in plotting to kill the king. Then, calling upon Ariel to fetch him his hat and rapier from the cell, Prospero attires himself as he once used to be in Milan. Sending Ariel to the king's ship to fetch the master and boatswain, he releases the king and lords from the spell and presents himself to them as Prospero, the Duke of Milan, so that they might recognise him. Alonso begs forgiveness, surrendering back to Prospero his suzerainty over the dukedom of Milan. Prospero embraces Gonzalo. Then, forgiving Antonio, his brother, he demands his dukedom back, which he knows his brother must surrender to him. Prospero then invites the group to look into his cell, to see a wonder. He reveals to their amazed gaze Miranda and Ferdinand playing chess together, during which Miranda forgives in advance any falseness that Ferdinand, despite his denial, might play.

Ferdinand is joyfully reunited with his father, explaining how he has chosen Miranda for his wife and been accepted. Alonso asks his son and Miranda for forgiveness. Gonzalo asks the gods for a blessing on the couple and calls on all to rejoice 'beyond a common joy', and to set down a record of this marvel 'with gold on lasting pillars', where in one voyage Claribel found a husband at Tunis, Ferdinand her brother found a wife where he himself was lost, Prospero found his dukedom in a poor isle, and all of them found themselves when no man was his own. Led by Alonso, they wish the couple joy.

Ariel returns with the master and boatswain, who reveal that the ship is not only unharmed but as good as when they first put out to sea. Alonso, trebly amazed, declares that some oracle must rectify their lack of knowledge, to which Prospero replies that he will explain all at more leisure.

Prospero then commands Ariel to set Caliban and his companions free. They enter, driven by Ariel and wearing their stolen apparel. Declaring their sin, Prospero gives over the butler and jester to the king and lords, but receives and acknowledges Caliban, 'this thing of darkness', as his own. He tells Caliban to go to the cell with his two companions and to trim it handsomely, if he wishes to receive Prospero's pardon. Caliban accepts this command and declares that he will be wise hereafter and seek for grace, acknowledging that he has been a thrice-double ass to take the drunken Stephano for a god and to worship the dull fool Trinculo. Alonso commands his servants to return the stolen clothing to where they found it. When this is done, Prospero invites the king and his followers into his poor cell, to take their rest for the night and to hear the story of his life on the island, ready for leaving the next morning for Naples and the wedding of Ferdinand and Miranda.

Finally, Prospero tells Ariel to ensure calm seas, good winds and swift sailing for them on the morrow, so that they may catch up with the royal fleet, after which Ariel is to be free.

Epilogue

Prospero concludes the play by explaining to the audience that his charms are all overthrown and that whatever strength he has left is but his own, which is faint. He asks to be released from his bands with the help of the audience's good hands and gentle breath, or else his project fails— which is to please. He no longer has spirits to enforce his will, or Art to enchant, and so his ending is despair unless relieved by prayer, which has the power to pierce and assault mercy itself and thereby free all faults. Just as each member of the audience would like to receive pardon for their crimes, so Prospero asks the audience for forgiveness of his so that he might be set free.

3. The Mysteries

To fully understand *The Tempest* it is fundamental to realise that Shakespeare has written a Mystery play, one that is based upon the Classical Mysteries of initiation. So, before analysing the play, let us look at the significance of this.

Æneas

Virgil's *Æneid*, particularly Books III and VI, provide a basic foundation for *The Tempest*. The *Æneid*, which in turn is based on Homer's *Odyssey* concerning the adventures of Ulysses, describes the adventures of Æneas, prince of Troy. In Book III is the basis for the banquet in *The Tempest*, whilst Book VI of the *Æneid* deals exclusively with the Mysteries of initiation and provides the main elements and purpose of Shakespeare's story. Virgil, as an initiate, was not permitted to openly reveal the Mysteries to the uninitiated, but he was allowed to present them in an allegory—which is exactly what Shakespeare does in *The Tempest*.

In Book III of the *Æneid* Virgil writes about the visit of Æneas to the Isles of the Strophads, where the harpies snatch away the food. This is echoed again in Book VI, although in a different context:-

> And full in their view are banquets furnished out with regal magnificence; the chief of Furies sits by them, and

debars them from touching the provisions with their
hands; and starts up, lifting her voice on high, and thunders over them with her voice.[1]

The harpy, described as a fury, goes on to do exactly
what Ariel does, when he thunders out his denunciation of
the 'three men of sin' (III, iii, 54-82). The banquet is a part of
the Mysteries of initiation, from which are excluded all those
who are 'at enmity with their brothers, had beaten a parent,
or wrought deceit against a client'.[2]

Book VI of the *Æneid* describes how Æneas, after leaving
Sicily where he had buried his father, is driven by a storm
onto the coast of Africa, where he meets and is entertained by
Dido, Queen of Carthage. (For this Virgil compacts history to
suit his allegory.) Dido falls in love with Æneas and wishes to
marry him. The time comes, however, when Æneas is commanded by the gods to leave Carthage with his followers and
continue on to Italy to make his new settlement there.

In his voyage from Carthage Æneas is driven by a second storm and shipwrecked upon the coast of Sicily. He is led
from thence to Cumæ, on the coast of Euboia (not far from
Naples), from whence the Sybil conducts him to the Infernal
Regions so that he might hear from his father (*via* the oracle)
concerning the fates that attend him and his posterity. Virgil
has this to say about the Underworld:-

The centaurs harbour at the Gates, and double-formed
Scyllas, the hundred-fold Briareus, the Snakes of Lerna,
hissing dreadfully, and Chimæra armed with flames, the
Gorgons and the Harpies, and the shades of three-bodied
form.

Before the entrance itself, and in the first jaws of Hell,
Grief and vengeful Cares have placed their couches; pale
Diseases inhabit there, and sad Old Age, and Fear, and
Want, evil goddess of persuasion, and unsightly

Poverty—forms too terrible to contemplate! And there, too, are Death and Toil; then Sleep, akin to Death, and evil Delights of mind; and upon the opposite threshold are seen death-bringing War, and the iron marriage-couches of the Furies, and raving Discord, with her viper-hair bound with gory wreaths. In the midst, an Elm dark and huge expands its boughs and aged limbs; making an abode which vain Dreams are said to haunt, and under whose every leaf they dwell.

As he is led through the tortuous underground passages and caverns, Æneas undergoes drowsiness and perceives the shades of the dead; but his guide, Charon, hastens him through safely:-

Here to reside delusive shades delight;
For nought dwells here but sleep and drowsy night.

Compare these descriptions with the following passages from *The Tempest*:-

Seb.   What a strange drowsiness possesses them!
Ant.   It is the quality o' the climate.[3]

Gon.   By'r lakin, I can go no further, sir;
      My old bones ache: here's a maze trod, indeed,
      Through forth-rights and meanders! By your patience,
      I must needs rest me.[4]

Finally Æneas emerges into the sunshine, in the midst of delightful meadows and happy people. Here, in the Elysian Fields, he is granted celestial visions.

This is the conclusion of the Mysteries in which Æneas was initiated. The historical-allegorical epilogue to the story relates how Æneas proceeded on to Italy and the Tiber, which he reached after a journey of seven years and the loss of thirteen ships. There Latinus, the king of the country, received him with great hospitality. Æneas married Latinus' daughter, Lavinia, and succeeded his father-in-law on the throne. From them were descended the Romans.

Dido

When Æneas met Queen Dido, she was already a widow. She was originally known as Elissa, daughter of Belus, king of Tyre, and was married to Sichæus, priest of Hercules at Tyre. Pygmalion, who succeeded to the throne of Tyre upon the death of Belus, murdered Elissa's husband in order to acquire his immense wealth. Heart-broken, Elissa left Tyre in search of a new settlement together with a number of Tyrians who likewise found the rule of Pygmalion odious. Eventually her fleet was driven by storm upon the shores of Africa, where she prevailed upon the inhabitants to allow her to buy as much land as she could enclose with a bull's hide, cut into thongs. Upon this piece of land she built a citadel, called Byrsa.

In the course of time the population increased, commerce flourished, and the boundaries of the city and surrounding land were enlarged. Her beauty and wisdom and the fame of her enterprise spread abroad, and many were her suitors. Her subjects wished her to marry Iarbas, king of Mauritania, who threatened war on the city. Elissa begged three months to consider before giving a decisive answer. During that time she built a funeral pyre, as if wishing to appease the *manes* (spirit) of Sichæus, to whom she had promised eternal fidelity. When all was prepared, she mounted the pyre and stabbed herself in front of her people. Her body was consumed in the flames.

Afterwards, because of her sacrificial act of fidelity, Elissa became known as Dido, her name concealing a secret sound and meaning. To the secret societies, such as the Dionysian

Artificers, she was known as Widow Dido, and all initiates of the Mysteries were referred to as sons of the widow. Since allegorically Dido was the personification of wisdom, the initiatic title also meant 'son of wisdom'.[5] She and the Tyrians were Phoenicians, and it may well be that the allegory of the phoenix rising from the ashes of its own pyre has a connection with Dido's self-immolation.

Virgil's allegorical history makes Dido live in the time of Æneas and commit suicide upon the pyre because of the sudden departure of Æneas, to whom she was seemingly married. Æneas thus became the 'Widower Æneas' in serious jest.

Byrsa became known as Carthage. It was destroyed by the Arabs in the 7th century, and Tunis, situated just ten miles away, later became the capital of the country. About this Adrian in *The Tempest* is actually more knowledgeable than the self-assured but mistaken Gonzalo:-

> Adr. 'Widow Dido' said you? you make me study of
> that: she was of Carthage, not of Tunis.
> *Gon.* This Tunis, sir, was Carthage.
> *Adr.* Carthage?
> *Gon.* I assure you, Carthage.[6]

The Blessed Isles

The whole setting of *The Tempest* is upon a magic isle surrounded by sea. Like the islands of the Bermudas, storms of thunder and lightning rage around its shores, yet it's interior is calm and peaceful. It is filled with spirits—strange sounds, voices, winds and shapes. It is set apart from the rest of the world, uninhabited except for the castaways. To have reached this island paradise they had to undergo shipwreck and an experience of death—psychological even if not actually physical, including a dying to their old way of life.

The Wisdom of Shakespeare in *The Tempest*

Shakespeare's description of the island and the ship-wreck is derived mainly from that of the Bermudas and the shipwreck of the Sea-Adventure. It also has links with the Isle of Man, named after the sea god Manannan[7] and considered to be a paradise by the Gaels, with its rocky island, the Calf of Man, lying off its storm-swept south coast. Prospero even embodies some of the attributes of Manannan, who was an illusionist and shape-shifter, a skilled sailor who sailed in boats needing neither oars nor sails to propel them, a creator of storms designed to wreck ships, an owner of a pack of hounds who chased boar into lakes, and a psychopomp who gave mortals a preview of the Otherworld by conducting them there for a time. But Prospero's island is neither the Bermudas nor Man. If the island's probable position were to be worked out on a map with respect to the story of the king's party sailing *en route* from Tunis to Naples when they were shipwrecked, then the island might possibly lie somewhere to the west or south-west of Naples, a metropolis associated in Classical times with a famous Mystery school of initiation (at Cumæ, near Naples).

This imaginary setting of Shakespeare's is a fine descrip-tion of the fabled Isles of the Blessed, the abode of souls who have died. The islands are said to lie in the west because, using the symbolism of the sun's course, the west signifies the setting or end of a life-span, thus sleep or death; just as the east represents the rising or birth into a new day of life on earth for the soul. Allegorically, in the west is the land of the setting sun, the place we all go to in our sleep or when we die. This land beneath the western horizon is not a physical location but a place or condition of the soul. It exists meta-physically, in the subtle realms of the mind, as the Otherworld—although special islands like the Isle of Man were physical symbols of the real but subtle Isles of the Blessed.

The Mysteries

We do not have to experience the complete death of the physical body in order to experience death and what lies beyond. Death is part of the cycle of life—of any cycle of time. In the Mystery schools of Classical Greece, Rome, Egypt, Britain, *etc.*, psychological death was a recognised stage on the path of initiation. Death ends one cycle of experience and begins another. It is the womb in which and out of which we are reborn. Death, therefore, has always been seen as the Great Initiator and the Great Gateway. Our poets and mystics have described such an experience as the dark night of the soul, although it can be an illumined experience as well.

This land of death is also a land of life—an earthly paradise that is a gateway and ladder to a heavenly paradise and eternal life. But how it is experienced depends upon the purity and virtue, or otherwise, of the soul. Of course, a physical environment that is healthy, beautiful and vibrant with life is immensely important, but paradise as such is essentially a state of consciousness—and an earthly paradise is that blessed consciousness which we can develop whilst incarnate in a terrestrial body. The celebrated 5th century BC Theban poet, Pindar, for instance, described the Otherworld as the abode of souls where 'the lawless souls of those who die here forthwith suffer punishment, and some one beneath the earth, pronouncing sentence by stern necessity, judges the sinful deeds done in this realm of Zeus; but the good enjoy the sun's light both by day and night—while those who, through a threefold existence in the upper and lower worlds, have kept their souls pure from all sin, ascend the path of Zeus to the castle of Cronos, where ocean breezes blow around the Islands of the Blessed, and golden flowers glitter'.[8]

The magic of the Blessed Isles is such that it has the means to assist all souls to purify themselves and to raise themselves up to a better state of consciousness and being. It also contains those beings who can bestow the means upon every soul. This means is composed of the two great powers and qualities of mercy and justice: justice to right wrongs and cleanse the soul of evil tendencies, and mercy to forgive and raise the soul up to a higher level of consciousness and knowledge of truth, giving every soul the chance to try again and to do things better the next time.

For these reasons the Isles of the West were described as the Blessed Isles or Fortunate Isles. All traditional accounts share the same basic symbolism of the sacred and blessed isles in the west, but separate traditions also have their own individual symbols as well. The symbols that Shakespeare uses belong to the Arthurian and the Atlantean traditions, wherein the Blessed Isle is called Avalon (the Arthurian tradition) or Ogygia (the Atlantean tradition).

Avalon

Is-land means 'Sacred Land', and all sacred land was deemed to be surrounded by water, representing the waters of life out of which the sacred land or mountain rises, soaring towards heaven. *Avalon*, the name of the Arthurian island of the blessed, means 'the Island of Apples' (*Aval*, 'Apple'; *Yn*, 'Island'). Avalon is pictured as being filled with apple orchards, with Merlin seated amongst them. Every apple tree signifies a tree of knowledge, and every apple symbolises a rich store of knowledge. In other words, Avalon is identical with the Garden of Eden. In fact, the very word *Eden* can be found in the Celtic language as *Y-Don*, meaning 'Hill of the Lord', as in Hebrew. Shakespeare drew on this symbolism deliberately:-

> *Seb.* I think he will carry this island home in his
> pocket, and give it his son for an apple.

Ant.   And, sowing the kernels of it in the sea, bring
      forth more islands.[9]

Fer.   Let me live here forever;
      So rare a wonder'd father and a wise
      Makes this place Paradise.[10]

The colour of apples is normally a lovely green, often tinged with rosy red. The apple and the rose originate from the same primitive species, and even today one can still see the similarity between the five-petalled flowers of the wild rose and apple blossom. This is one of the reasons why the Blessed Isles are known as the Land of the Rosicrucians.

The rosy hue signifies love: the green colour is its counterbalance and represents purity and sincerity. Both colours are particularly associated with the heart. The Celts used this symbolism in a profound way. For instance, the Celtic word *glas* denotes green, especially in the sense of the vitality and ever-livingness of nature that we still call the 'greening' of nature today.

Gon.   How lush and lusty the grass looks! How green![11]

But whilst green is the outer colour, the inner colour of *glas* was understood as being blue—a colour that is clairvoyantly perceived to lie behind all other colours as the energetic colour of life itself, of which white is the reflection. *Glas* also denotes crystal and clarity, such that clear quartz crystal is a symbol of what *glas* means. From *glas* we derive our word *glass*, but we lose some of the deeper meaning in the translation, as the six-fold structure of quartz forms part of the original symbolism, and the chaotic structure of glass is simply not the same!

The whole island of Avalon is denoted by the word *glas*, as in *Glas-ton*, 'the Crystal Hill'. (The Celtic *ton* has the meaning of 'head hill' or 'hill of judgement and mercy', 'hill of the law', 'meeting hill' or 'hill of the Assembly'). Thus Avalon is known as the Crystal Mountain or Crystal Island, or simply as the Grass-green Island of Apples. It is also known as Merlin's Green Diamond or Emerald, which was perceived as clear crystal of a bluish colour, rather like Moses' Tablets of the Law which cabalistic tradition relates were made of sapphire written on with letters of fire. Merlin's crystal (which, it should be noted, is his sacred land) is also his Emerald Tablet (or Tablets), like those of Moses and Hermes Trismegistus. Merlin's island, which is the Blessed Isle, is said to be surrounded with mist, and in the centre is to be found the heart-shaped Glen of Precious Stones (or Rubies).

An old legend relates how a renowned Druid came to Avalon, which story enhances and helps to explain the background to Prospero's story from another point of view:–

> In former days there lived in Skerr a Druid of renown. He sat with his face to the west on the shore, his eye following the declining sun. As he sat musing on a rock, a storm arose on the sea; a cloud, under whose squally skirts the foaming waters tossed, rushed suddenly into the bay, and from its dark womb emerged a ship or boat with white sails bent to the wind, and banks of gleaming oars on either side. But it was destitute of Mariners, itself seeming to live and move. An unusual terror seized on the aged Druid; he heard a voice call 'Arise, and see the Green Isle of those who have passed away!' Then he entered the vessel. Immediately the wind shifted, the cloud enveloped him, and in the bosom of the vapour he sailed away. Seven days gleamed on him through the mist; on the eighth the waves rolled violently, the vessel pitched, and darkness thickened around him, when suddenly he heard a cry, 'The Isle! The Isle!' Before his eyes lay the Isle of the Departed.'[12]

The Mysteries

From this point of view the whole play can be taken as the psychological experience of one person, with all the characters in the story being aspects or sub-personalities of that person. All Shakespeare's plays can be taken in this way, providing deep psychological analysis of various possible states of the human soul, good and bad, and offering suggestions as how to deal with those states of consciousness. Likewise they can be taken as a study of human society, with that society being considered as one body, one soul, one group consciousness, with all its various aspects and members.

According to myth, when King Arthur was mortally wounded he was taken in a crystal boat by three women (*i.e.* the triple goddess) to Glaston, the Crystal Island. There he sleeps with his zodiac of knights, dead yet alive, awaiting the sound of the horn at sunrise to wake him up and bring him back into action in the world again.

The myth of Merlin recounts that the mage retired to the Crystal Island with his nine orders of bards and the thirteen treasures of Britain—the Grail treasures. On the sacred island he was initiated by his own master, *Prydydd Mawr*, 'the Great Bard', who revealed to Merlin a wonderful orchard that contained the secrets of earth and of planetary revolution. This orchard contained 'seven score and seven delicious apple trees of equal age, height, length and size, which sprang from the bosom of Mercy.'[13]

Besides orchards of apple trees, Avalon is said to contain oak trees and pines (or cedars). Furthermore, living in amongst these trees and rooting for acorns are swine, looked after by Merlin, their swineherd.

Just as the apple tree signifies the tree of knowledge of good and evil, so the oak tree is the emblem of the tree of life, or light, and is the counter-balance to the apple. Life is light, which is wisdom, whilst knowledge is intelligence. Wisdom and Intelligence are the two great principles that underlie

Mercy and Justice respectively, and they are represented by the oak and apple trees. For this reason the Druids conducted their ceremonies in sacred oak groves (as also did Abraham). Their title, Druid (*Druithin*) means 'Servant of Truth', and one of the derivations of *Druithin* is from *Duir*, meaning 'oak'. Hence they were known as 'the men of the oaks'. This actually meant that a Druid, to be worthy of his title, was wise and merciful, with orchards of knowledge growing from his bosom of mercy. Merlin was a Druid. His master's name was *Blaize*, which simply means 'the Great Light' (*i.e.* 'Blaze'), the Wisdom of God.

This emphasis on Mercy, and on the Wisdom which underlies Mercy, is of paramount importance. It is a major theme of *The Tempest*, just as it is the major theme of the myth of Avalon. In Shakespeare's story many people lie in the power of Prospero. It is essential that he learns to develop mercy—not just to feel it or know it intellectually, but to put it into practice. Only by doing this can he attain to the full status of a Druid, a Servant of Truth—a Master.

> *Ari.* ...Your charm so strongly works 'em
> That if you now beheld them, your affections
> Would become tender.
> *Pros.* Dost thou think so, spirit?
> *Ari.* Mine would, sir, were I human.
> *Pros.* And mine shall.
> Hast thou, which art but air, a touch, a feeling
> Of their afflictions, and shall not myself,
> One of their kind, that relish all as sharply
> Passion as they, be kindlier mov'd than thou art?
> Though with their high wrongs I am struck to th' quick,
> Yet with my nobler reason 'gainst my fury
> Do I take part: the rarer action is
> In virtue than in vengeance: they being penitent,
> The sole drift of my purpose doth extend
> Not a frown further. Go release them, Ariel:

> My charms I'll break, their senses I'll restore,
> And they shall be themselves.[14]

> *Pros.…* I do forgive thee,
> Unnatural though thou art.[15]

> *Pros.* For you, most wicked sir, whom to call brother
> Would even infect my mouth, I do forgive
> Thy rankest fault,—all of them; and require
> My dukedom of thee, which perforce, I know,
> Thou must restore.[16]

Once the state of mercy is attained, it has a redeeming effect on others, even Caliban:-

> *Pros.…* Go, sirrah, to my cell;
> Take with you your companions; as you look
> To have my pardon, trim it handsomely.
> *Cal.* Ay, that I will; and I'll be wise hereafter,
> And seek for grace.[17]

The pine (or cedar, the 'royal' pine) completes the trinity of sacred trees in Avalon. The pine signifies the third tree, the balance and union of the other two, known in Cabala as the middle pillar topped by the Crown. On the topmost branches of the cedar sits the Phoenix, the king of the birds: but here we come into the mythology of Atlantis:-

> *Seb.* … Now I will believe
> That there are unicorns; that in Arabia
> There is one tree, the phoenix' throne; one phoenix
> At this hour reigning there.[18]

The Phoenix

The phoenix combines the symbolism of the eagle and the dove, both emblems of St John, with the dove being also the emblem of the Holy Spirit. The phoenix is essentially a dove—a white dove, signifying its utter purity, whose breast is turned a purple-red through the pouring out of its love to others. This purple-red colour of royal love is what is known as *phoenice*, which word also means 'beautiful'. Thus the phoenix is an emblem of beauty—the beauty of the true soul, who has been through and risen above death, reborn from its phoenix pyre. Shakespeare's mystical poem, *The Phoenix and Turtle,* is about this perfection.

When love pours out from the heart in compassion and service to others it becomes a light that illumines the mind and even the body. Simultaneously with this, the serpent-fire or *kundalini* rises up the spine and bursts through the crown of the head, forming the plume or crest of light seen above the heads of saints. This plume is known as the sign of the dove, equivalent to the trisül of Shiva in Vedic tradition. It is the crest of the phoenix. The eagle represents the stage of evolution immediately prior to the final attainment denoted by the dove-phoenix.

The eagle has piercing sight and can soar to the heights, and so for this reason the eagle signifies great perception, great judgement. But the eagle is a hunter and, specifically in symbolism, is the enemy and destroyer of the snake (like the Horus falcon in Egyptian symbolism). Mercy is even greater, and this the dove or phoenix represents. Shakespeare's plays are all concerned with the development (or rejection) of mercy amongst human beings. Some of Shakespeare's heroes, or more often heroines, are depicted as having attained a mastery of love. In *The Merchant of Venice*, for instance, Shakespeare shows mercy already embodied in Portia, the 'goddess' from Belmont (the Mount of Beauty), right at the start of the play. *The Tempest,* however, shows the gradual attainment of mercy in its fullness by an outstanding individual, after he has learnt how to master the more basic elements of nature by his practical knowledge of nature's laws. Prospero progresses from a knowledge and mastery of the lesser laws of nature to a knowledge and mastery of the greater laws, coming finally to that of the greatest law of all— the law of love. From being a judge, enforcing justice, he becomes a king, bestowing mercy.

The play is, therefore, nothing more or less than a theatrical exposition on the great theme being promulgated by Francis Bacon at that time, and a commentary on the biblical declaration that mankind's birthright was to have power and lordship over nature:-

> So God created man in His own image, in the image of God created He him; male and female created He them. And God blessed them, and God said unto them, 'Be fruitful and multiply, and replenish the earth, and subdue it: and have dominion over the fish of the sea, and over the fowl of the air, and over every living thing that moveth upon the earth.[19]

But, as Bacon carefully pointed out, this dominion is only achieved by serving nature: that is to say, by discovering and using nature's laws, and ultimately nature's supreme law, which is love, for charitable purposes:-

> Now the empire of man over things is founded on the Arts and Sciences only; for Nature is only governed by obedience… Only let man regain his right over Nature, which belongs to him by the gift of God; let there be given to him the power: right reason and sound religion will teach him how to apply it.[20]

> In sum, I would advise all in general, that they would take into serious consideration the true and genuine ends of knowledge; that they seek it not either for pleasure, or contention, or contempt of others, or for profit, or fame, or for honour and promotion, or such like adulterate or infe-

rior ends; but for the merit and emolument of life; and that they regulate and perfect the same in charity. For the desire of power was the fall of angels, the desire of knowledge the fall of man; but in charity there is no excess, neither man nor angels ever incurred danger by it.[21]

Prospero was noted for his knowledge of the liberal arts, but he needed to learn how to apply it:-

> *Pros.* And Prospero the prime duke, being so reputed
> In dignity, and for the liberal Arts
> Without a parallel; those being all my study...[22]

One exquisite passage on mercy from *The Merchant of Venice* is worth quoting here, as this is the lesson Prospero is learning on his magic isle:-

> *Por.* The quality of mercy is not strain'd,
> It droppeth as the gentle rain from heaven
> Upon the place beneath; it is twice blest,
> It blesseth him that gives, and him that takes,
> 'Tis mightiest in the mightiest, it becomes
> The throned monarch better than his crown.
> His sceptre shows the force of temporal power,
> The attribute to awe and majesty,
> Wherein doth sit the dread and fear of kings,
> It is an attribute of God himself;
> And earthly power doth then show likest God's
> When mercy seasons justice: therefore Jew,
> Though justice be thy plea, consider this,
> That in the course of justice, none of us
> Should see salvation: we do pray for mercy,
> And that same prayer, doth teach us all to render the deeds of mercy.[23]

This Prospero learns, this he acquires, and for this he prays.

The Phoenix is the title of the great King of Atlantis and his Queen. The King of Atlantis was Atlas, also known as Enoch ('the Great Initiate'). Enoch was the first great initiate, master and teacher on earth who 'walked with God'[24] and was 'translated' (*i.e.* resurrected) body and soul into the highest heaven,[25] where, as Rabbinical tradition records, he became the Archangel Metatron. His continuing role is to purify, initiate and teach mankind, and thereby prepare the way for the Messiah, for which purpose he reincarnates from time to time. (As such he is said to have been both Elijah and John the Baptist, heralds of the Christ.)

Ogygia

Atlantis, meaning 'Land risen above the Waters', is described in legend as having been comprised of a central part plus a great continent which lay to its west. It is a land which is periodically destroyed but which rises again. It is the central part that is considered sacred. This heartland is divided symbolically into ten islands—three large ones and seven smaller ones, on the cabalistic pattern of the Tree of Life with its ten principles. The three larger islands are sacred to (1) Ammon and Hera, (2) Poseidon and Demeter, and (3) Hades and Hestia. The seven smaller islands are all sacred to Persephone, the daughter of Zeus and Demeter.

The ten sacred islands of Atlantis were known under the name of Ogygia, and were said to lie due west, beneath the setting sun. Youths and maidens dance hand in hand in the dewy grass in Ogygia. Green trees are laden with apples. One of the orchards is the famous Garden of the Hesperides, with its golden apples. A palace of glass floats in the air, receiving the souls of the blessed. It is the place of the Golden Age.

In esoteric tradition Ammon, Poseidon and Hades are each known as being aspects of the great god Zeus (Jupiter), the 'Father of Light', who is thereby a Trinity. Hera, Demeter and Hestia are his triune feminine counterparts. All kings of Atlantis are, therefore, imbued with the qualities and powers of Zeus, wielding the thunderbolt and lightning rod, cleaving oaks (which are sacred to Zeus), and governing their realm and all its inhabitants with magical power and authority. In *The Tempest* Prospero is given by Shakespeare all the fundamental qualities of a king of Atlantis:-

> *Mir.* If by your Art, my dearest father, you have
> put the wild waters in this roar, allay them.
> The sky, it seems, would pour down stinking pitch,
> But that the sea, mounting to th' welkin's cheek,
> Dashes the fire out.[26]

In the wonderful and most moving declaration of Prospero's, in which he says farewell to his 'rough magic' in order to find a greater magic, Prospero's association with Jupiter, the god of the island, is made very clear:-

> *Pros.* Ye elves of hills, brooks, standing lakes and groves;
> And ye that on the sands with printless foot
> Do chase the ebbing Neptune, and do fly him
> When he comes back: you demi-puppets that
> By moonshine do the green sour ringlets make,
> Whereof the ewe not bites: and you whose pastime
> Is to make midnight mushrooms, that rejoice
> To hear the solemn curfew; by whose aid
> (Weak masters though ye be) I have bedimm'd
> The noontide sun, call'd forth the mutinous winds,
> And 'twixt the green sea and the azur'd vault
> Set roaring war: to the dread rattling thunder
> Have I given fire, and rifted *Jove's* stout oak
> With his own bolt: the strong-bas'd promontory
> Have I made shake, and by the spurs pluck'd up
> The pine and cedar: graves at my command
> Have wak'd their sleepers, op'd, and let 'em forth

> By my so potent Art. But this rough magic
> I here abjure: and when I have requir'd
> Some heavenly music (which even now I do)
> To work mine end upon their senses, that
> This airy charm is for, I'll break my staff,
> Bury it certain fadoms in the earth,
> And deeper than did ever plummet sound
> I'll drown my book.[27]

This speech appears to be based on a passage appearing in Ovid's *Metamorphosis*, being an incantation by Medea.[28] But Shakespeare has adapted it, omitting what might be called the darker aspects, retaining only the 'white' magic and adding to it the attributes of Jupiter.

The incantation involves the lesser spirits of nature. What Prospero possessed—or rather, was able to command—was a spirit that Medea could never invoke or control. This spirit is that which is called Ariel. Ben Jonson, in his satire on Shakespeare's *Tempest* and the Rosicrucians, which he entitled *The Fortunate Isles and their Union*, parodies Ariel very pointedly as Jophiel, 'an aery spirit, and (according to the Magi) the Intelligence of Jupiter's sphere':-

> *Joh.*   Like a lightning from the sky,
>   Or an arrow shot by Love,
>   Or a bird of his let fly.
>   Bee't a sparrow or a dove:
>   With that winged haste, come I,
>   Loosed from the sphere of Jove
>   To wish good-night
>   To your delight.[29]

What is not so clear in the Shakespeare play is made clearer by Jonson. In particular Jonson not only names Ariel as the 'Intelligence of Jupiter's sphere' but also identifies Ariel's symbolic bird-form as a sparrow or a dove.

The dove, which is the same as the phoenix, is the emblem of the Holy Spirit. The sparrow, far from being a mundane symbol, is complementary to the dove imagery: for, in the well-known nursery rhyme, it is the sparrow that shoots the arrow at cock robin and pierces poor robin's breast. Robin is the name of the king who dies for the good of his people, or the initiate who dies (metaphorically) for the good of others (*e.g.* Robin Hood). The robin's red breast symbolises his heart love (blood) poured out for others, like the phoenix. What pierces his heart in order to allow the love to flow is love, for the arrow symbolises the ray of love that is shot by Cupid from the bow of the heart. In other words the common, seemingly insignificant sparrow was used as a symbol for Cupid, the divine love-wisdom or Word of God. Thus Ariel is identified as being both the intelligence (robin) and the love-wisdom (sparrow) of God.

Prospero alludes to this by referring to Ariel as his 'bird', his 'chick' and his 'Spirit':-

Pros. Spirit, We must prepare to meet with Caliban.[30]

Pros. This was well done, my bird.[31]

Pros. My Ariel, chick...[32]

Through the use of this symbolic imagery the relationship of Ariel to Prospero should become clear, for Ariel is Prospero's 'chick'. Ariel is hatched out of Prospero. Moreover, Ariel gradually grows up as the play progresses, until the time comes for him to be released from the nest.

Cabalistically, Jupiter signifies the Grace or Mercy of God. At the very end of the play Prospero finally achieves all of what Jupiter means, and therefore what a king of Atlantis should be, by freeing Ariel, by forgiving all the other characters and treating them kindly yet wisely, not without power, and then by calling forth the qualities of love and forgiveness in all of us in his final speech to us, the audience:–

> *Pros.* And my ending is despair,
>   Unless I be reliev'd by prayer
>   Which pierces so, that it assaults
>   Mercy itself, and frees all faults.
>   As you from crimes would pardon'd be,
>   Let your indulgence set me free.[33]

The imagery of prayer piercing and assaulting mercy is derived from the Cupid and sparrow symbolism: for Cupid's arrow signifies a ray of love shot from the bow of a loving heart. Such is true prayer, which awakens (or 'assaults') mercy. It is then the Jovan mercy that has the power to free all faults and set Prospero free.

Freedom in the Mystery teachings has two stages, associated with two Greek words: αγνον, meaning 'pure' or 'free from evil', and οσιωθειξ, meaning 'set free' or 'consecrated'. The former relates to the completion of the Lesser Mysteries of initiation, the latter to the final accomplishment of the Greater Mysteries. The release of Ariel from the pine, and thus from the clutches of the evil witch Sycorax, relates to the first freeing, whilst the setting free of Ariel from Prospero's service at the end of the play relates to the second.

Jupiter is associated with the number 12, it being the approximate number of years of its sidereal cycle.[34] As a representative of Jupiter, these twelve-year cycles are important in the life of an Atlantean lord on his sacred island, and govern all who live therein:-

> *Pros.* [Sycorax] did confine thee,
>   By help of her more potent ministers,
>   And in her most unmitigable rage,

> Into a cloven pine; within which rift
> Imprison'd thou didst painfully remain
> A dozen years…[35]

> *Pros.* If thou more murmur'st, I will rend an oak,
> And peg thee in his knotty entrails, till
> Thou hast howl'd away twelve winters.[36]

> *Pros.* Twelve year since, Miranda, twelve year since,
> Thy father was the Duke of Milan, and
> A prince of power.[37]

The number twelve is also associated with the Zodiac, with its twelve signs and influences through which the sun moves on its annual course in company with the planets.

The Great Lord of the Zodiac is Cronos (Saturn), the divine father of Zeus (Jupiter). He is the archetype of King Arthur. Together with his 'queen', the great goddess Rhea, Cronos rules the Round Table of space and time. He is the Time Lord. He rules all and is the Spirit of all Nature. For this reason the ancients called him *Pan*, which means 'All'. The great god Pan is the god of Nature, the god of all manifested life, the supreme god of Atlantis, Avalon and Arcadia. In the Atlantean tradition he is said to sleep in Ogygia, guarded by Briareces. He is Lord of the Golden Age with which Atlantis is associated. The Golden Age recurs periodically whenever Cronos (*i.e.* Pan) awakens and openly rules the epoch. Gonzalo briefly parodies this on the shores of the island, to the merriment of the others:-

> *Gon.* I would with such perfection govern, sir,
> T' excel the Golden Age.[38]

To right wrongs, to better things, to raise all human beings to a higher level of civilisation, to prosper them and, all in all, to help usher in a golden age, is the purpose of Prospero and the story of this superb play.

4. Ariel

Just as we need to understand that *The Tempest* is a Mystery play, with images taken from the Classical, Phoenician and Druidic Mysteries, we also need to understand something about Ariel before proceeding any further: for the name and character of Ariel contains a key to the whole play. Without Ariel, Prospero can perform none of his magic. Without Ariel, there would be no *Tempest*. In Ariel, Shakespeare has placed a great secret. He has chosen the name of Ariel carefully, and made use of Ariel's many levels of meaning, superimposing and weaving them together to create a play with many layers of hidden truths behind the outermost form.

An Airy Spirit

At the literal level of meaning, Ariel is a spirit released by Prospero from a cloven pine, in which he had been imprisoned by the 'foul witch Sycorax' for a dozen years (I, ii, 258-292). He had been shut in the pine because he refused to carry out the abhorrent commands of Sycorax. In return for his liberty Ariel served Prospero for another twelve years, which would have been thirteen years had not the events of *The Tempest* taken place. After these events Ariel is given his full freedom, as promised by Prospero.

Ariel is referred to as 'an ayrie spirit' in the 'Names of the Actors' prefixed to the play in the Shakespeare Folio. He is sensitive, moody and compassionate, and obeys Prospero's commands. However, he carries out those commands in ways that he thinks best, and sometimes thinks ahead of Prospero, anticipating Prospero's needs and acting independently to fulfil those needs (*e.g.* when he leads the servants into the foul smelling lake).

Ariel can be visible or invisible to the eye, but he remains invisible (except to Prospero) during the course of the play's action, except for the one moment when he takes on the form of a harpy and appears as such to the lords. He is heard, though, as music or a strange humming, felt as a breath or wind, and smelt as a sweet air or fragrance.

As an intelligence (*i.e.* spirit) he has a universal awareness of all that is happening or might happen. He understands the laws or causes of things and, as a superior 'law', he can affect and manipulate the lesser laws of nature as required. He is able to work upon the phenomenal world of the elements with ease, moulding or turning them to whatever is required, and is at home in any of the four elements—earth, water, air or fire. Not only this, but he also has the power to work on people's minds and imagination, to lead them, chase them, frighten them, make suggestions, or even to inspire and teach them, as he does with Prospero when he suggests that Prospero's affections should become tender and inspires Prospero to be merciful (v, i, 7-33).

Although in fact Ariel never tells lies, Prospero at one point charges Ariel with lying; but this is more to do with Prospero's own inner tension and anxiety than a true comment on Ariel's character. In this scene (I, ii, 242-297) Ariel acts as the Initiator and Tester, testing Prospero's own vows and memory, only to be unjustly condemned by Prospero in a typical human reaction:-

> *Pros.*   Thou liest, malignant thing; hast thou forgot the
>   fowle witch Sycorax...? [1]

Ariel

Ariel, of course, has not forgotten Sycorax; but Prospero's reaction must run its course, whilst Ariel refuses to speak ill and be drawn into an argument detrimental to love.

> *Ariel.*   Pardon, master:
>   I will be correspondent to command,
>   And do my spriting gently.[2]

Ariel is the perfect servant. Yet it is he alone who has the power to do the work requested of him, and he is the one who does it. Without Ariel, Prospero's own personal power or strength is, as he himself admits at the end, 'most faint' (Epilogue, line 3). So who is the real master?

The clue to this lies in Ariel's name, the meanings of which are as follows:-

Lion of God

The Hebrew word *Ariel* means 'Lion of God', which is an ancient title for Jerusalem. *Jeru-salem* (or *Hiero-Salem*) means 'The Great Peace' or 'Holy Place of Solomon' (*Solomon* means 'peace'). According to astrological and hermetic symbolism, the lion rules the heart wherein burns the fire of love, the fire of peace. The lion signifies the spirit and the courage of the heart, which is unshakeable faith, the foundation of all that is good. This faith is essentially love, the spirit of the heart, which is peaceful and bestows peace. Jerusalem is the name of the heart chakra in Western lore, which is why the tribes of Israel built their capital city of Jerusalem at the heart centre of their country, and why the city lay in the tribal land of Judah—Judah's symbol being the lion. The lion is also the epithet of the Messiah or Christ, the King of the Jews (*i.e.* the tribe of Judah), whose throne and palace is in Jerusalem, the heart.

Hearth and Heart of God

Ariel also means 'Hearth of God'. The hearth, upon which burns the sacred fire of the home, was originally built in the centre or heart of the house. It still is considered the heart of every home. The hearthstone signifies the heart, on (or in) which burns the fire that warms and illumines, bringing life and joy to the home. The fire itself is an emblem of love. The word *hearth* is kin to the word *heart* for this reason, with the aspirate 'h' being considered a 'breath' rather than a letter.

Archangel Auriel

Ariel is an alternative spelling for the name *Auriel*, the modern spelling of which is Uriel.[3] In Hebraic and Christian Cabala Auriel is the name of the Archangel of Grace or Goodwill, one of the Seven Great Spirits that stand before the Throne of God. This archangel is the spiritual intelligence or 'form' (*i.e.* archetype) of the sweet emotion, goodwill and friendship of God. That is to say, Auriel is the spiritual expression of the divine principle known as *Netzach* ('Victory' or 'Grace'), which inspires in us unselfish, loving qualities and an artistic nature. The archetype is represented by the goddess Venus, or Aphrodite. This spiritual intelligence manifests in the human soul as human desire and passion of an unselfish kind, and can develop into a powerful expression of love. Its negative counterpart is selfish desire and lust, as represented to some extent by the Venus of Shakespeare's poem, *Venus and Adonis*, until her lust is turned to love by the death of Adonis.

Just as *Netzach*'s higher counterpart is *Chesed* ('Mercy, Compassion, Benevolence, Generosity, Forgiveness'), so Auriel's higher counterpart is the Archangel Zadkiel, the archetype of *Chesed*. *Chesed*, like *Netzach*, is also known as the

Grace of God, but mercy is a higher, more powerful and more universal grace than simple goodwill. *Chesed* is sometimes referred to simply as 'Love', since mercy or compassion is often perceived as being the highest possible expression of love. Jupiter, or Zeus, is the Classical representation of the archetype of Mercy. His name means 'Father of Light', for the radiance of love (*i.e.* mercy) is light.

So, when Ben Jonson parodied Ariel under the name of Jophiel in his masque, *The Fortunate Isles and their Union,* and referred to Jophiel as being 'the intelligence of Jupiter's sphere' and 'an arrow shot by Love', he was being accurate from the Cabalistic point of view. The ancient symbol of the heart is a bow (*e.g.* as in Ancient Egyptian hieroglyphics), whilst the arrow signifies a ray of love-light shot from that bow of Love. In other words, Ariel is a ray of the general radiance of Zadkiel, whilst Zadkiel is the radiance of Divine Love, the Logos, signified by the Greeks as Eros and the Romans as Cupid, the Eldest or First-born of God.

Auriel is said to rule the north, the earth, midnight and midwinter. These four are associated with the light-source or 'star' which is born in the heart of everything—in the heart of darkness, of matter, *etc.,*—and which is the Alpha and Omega of all light and life. The North Pole Star, the Blazing Star or Star of Bethlehem, the Christ child born in the cave at Christmas, the golden seed sown in the ground over winter and which germinates at midwinter, are all symbols of what Auriel signifies or is associated with. Auriel is also said to rule over nature and the elements of nature, and in this respect one can often find Venus depicted as the goddess of nature.

Venus' special day is Friday. Friday is the Day of Friendship and Day of Freedom; for the word *Fri-day* means 'Love-day'. *Fri* is derived from the Sanskrit word *pri,* signifying 'love', and our words *free, friendship* and *freedom* are based on this root. Friday is the day of the Last Supper, an intimate sacred meal based upon the Hebrew *Qadosh*—the Feast of Brotherhood that is partaken between friends on the night of (*i.e.* before) the Passover,[4] in which the bread and wine of the Mysteries is blessed and shared. The *agape* ('love-feast') of the Greek Christians and the banquet of the Mysteries represent the same feast of love. When the banquet in *The Tempest* appears, it is impossible for the 'three men of sin' to partake of it, for they are not in the state of purity, love and friendship required. Ariel, who is *a priori* the angel of the banquet, appears to them instead as a harpy, protecting the sanctity of the feast and bringing to their attention their state of impurity and unfitness for the feast (III, iii, 18-82).

The Quintessence

Ariel is at home in all the natural elements and can appear as any of them, yet at the same time he is more than any of them. He rules the earth, yet can fly in the air, swim in the water and dive into the fire. He is master of them all and can take on the nature of any one of them. This is a description of the alchemical quintessence, æther. This quintessence is known as the shape-shifting Mercury, or Quicksilver. Mercury is described by the alchemists as being tricksy (*i.e.* full of tricks, playful, but also difficult to handle because so subtle, having a quicksilver-like tendency to run everywhere and escape); hence Prospero addresses Ariel as 'My tricksey Spirit' (V, i, 227).

The quintessence is often represented by spiritual Air, signified by the Hebrew letter *Aleph* ('A'), which is associated with the heart of man. The description of Ariel as an 'airy spirit' is therefore exact, but it is not the elemental air of the corporeal or even the psychological world that is being referred to, but the ætheric Air of the spiritual realms.

Hebraic tradition teaches that spiritual Air is composed

of two aspects or poles: (1) spiritual Water, represented by the letter *Mem* ('M'), and (2) spiritual Fire, represented by the letter *Shin* ('Sh'), the union of which forms spiritual Air or Mercury. Another Hebraic name for this 'airy' quintessence is *Shamaim,* a word compounded of *Shin* and *Mem.* From this *Shamaim* or Æther the heavens are formed. In Alchemy it is known as the Universal Agent and Powder of Projection.

Because it is formed of spiritual Fire and Water, the Mercurial quintessence is sometimes designated as 'Fire-Water', or as 'the Water that does not wet', or 'the Fire that does not burn'. These latter two metaphors are used during the actual storm of *The Tempest,* for Ariel 'flames' all over the ship like St Elmo's fire (I, i, 198), and at the same time is the 'foaming brine' that is 'all afire' with him, into which the occupants of the vessel plunge (I, ii, 210-212), only to discover, on arrival on the island, that their clothes are dry and 'rather new-dyed than stained with salt water' (II, i: 60).

Hermes Trismegistus

St Elmo's fire is known as St Hermes' fire, Hermes being a Greek name for Mercury. Hermes' title, 'Trismegistus' ('Thrice-greatest'), refers to the spiritual Fire, Water and Air of which he is composed, and to the principles which lie behind them.

Hermes is the conductor of souls through the underworld, leading them through experiences of purgatory, repentance, purification and initiation, and ultimately taking them, if possible, right up to the Throne of God. He is accompanied by his dog—the 'watch-dog' (I, ii, 385) that guards the sacred heart and Mystery. In Egyptian myth this dog is Anubis, who guards the Truth and weighs the heart of each individual person in the balance in the Hall of Judgement, to see whether the heart be true or not. Ariel's song (I, ii, 377-

389) brings in both the 'watchdog' and the 'chanticleer' (cockerel), signifying the Guardian of Truth and the Teacher of Truth, which are two principal aspects of Hermes.

> *Ariel.* [Song]…Hark, hark.
> *Refrain.* Bow-wow.
> *Ariel.* The watch dogs bark:
> *Refrain.* Bow-wow.
> *Ariel.* Hark, hark! I hear
>   The strain of strutting chanticleer.
> *Refrain.* Cock a diddle dow.[5]

Out of all the spiritual beings that exist, Mercury-Hermes is able to come and go as he pleases through all the spheres of existence, from the heights of heaven down to the depths of the underworld. In the Greek version of the myth of initiation, Hermes is the one who rescues Persephone from the phenomenal realm of nature, the sphere of Hades, and leads her back to the celestial realm of the soul, the sphere of Demeter. In this story Persephone is representative of the human soul or psyche.

Hermes teaches and guides, but he also, as part of the training and development of the soul, challenges and tests all who are following the path of life. That is to say, he deliberately leads astray those who are susceptible to being led astray, but only to purify and educate. Ferdinand follows Ariel as a sure and true guide straight to Prospero's cell, but the lords and servants are led by Ariel all over the island as if in a maze, until, like Alonso, they have undergone a 'sea-change' and are ready to come to Prospero's cell, the magical centre or heart of the island.

Hiram Abif

In the Ancient Chaldean version of the Emerald Tablet of Hermes Trismegistus, Hermes is referred to as *CHIRAM*

Ariel

TELAT MECHASOT – 'Chiram [the Universal Agent], One in essence but Three in aspect'.[6] *Chiram* is the original spelling of *Hiram*, as in Freemasonry's Hiram Abif. In fact Ariel and Hiram Abif, the Master Builder of King Solomon's Temple, are one and the same, when the deeper meaning of the Biblical story of Solomon's Temple is considered. (The Bible has four basic levels of meaning: (1) *Pshat*, the literal meaning, (2) *Ramaz,* the metaphorical or moral meaning, (3) *Darash,* the 'homiletic truth' or metaphysical science, and (4) *Sod,* the 'Mystery' or secret magic.)

Chiram is derived from the three Hebrew letters, *Cheth* ('Ch'), *Resh* ('R') and *Mem* ('M').[7] These three consonants stand for *Chamah*, *Ruach* and *Majim*, which describe the three spiritual elements of Fire (*Shin*), Air (*Aleph*) and Water (*Mem*) as 'invisible light or fire', 'spirit, air or wind' and 'water or condensed air' respectively. In the Hermetic teachings these are represented by the spiritual Sun, Mercury and Moon respectively—the Sun being the 'Father', the Moon being the 'Mother' and Mercury being their 'Son'.

Chiram's title, *Abif,* is derived from *Abba* ('Father') and is a courtesy title meaning 'my Father': for Chiram, as the quintessence, is the 'Father' of the four alchemical elements of the psyche and nature. This is the second Father, the first being the Fire or spiritual Sun (*Chamah-Shin*) The second Father is associated with Jupiter (*Hu-Pater*), the 'Father of Light' that is the Mercy or Grace of Love.

Whereas the first Father is what Freemasonry refers to as 'the Lost Word', which every Freemason seeks to find, the second Father, Chiram, is the one who knows that Word and is willing to teach it to those who are ready. To discover the Word, we must first discover, raise and set free Chiram from the tomb in which he is buried. Jesus put it another way when he said, cryptically, 'I am the way, the truth, and the life: no man cometh unto the Father, but by me'.[8]

65

Freemasons honour their Father in their very name, for *free* means 'love' and *mason* means 'builder'. Chiram is the builder of love. Freemasons are training to be builders of love, by finding and releasing their Master and thereby being taught the Lost Word. In regard to this it should be noted that *The Tempest* is signed with the signature of Hiram Abif—the play's text beginning with 'Master' (unspoken) and ending with 'free' (spoken).

The Sound of Creation

Ariel performs his work exactly and quickly, in contradistinction to Caliban who is clumsy and slow. Ariel is industrious and tells no lies, whereas Caliban is lazy and does tell lies. Whilst Caliban uses language to curse, Ariel fills the atmosphere of the island with harmonious sounds.

These sounds are important. The lords hear them differently, either as sweet music or as a ditty (Ferdinand, Act I, ii), or as solemn music (the lords, Act II, i), or as a strange humming (Gonzalo, Act II, ii), or as harmonious and marvellous sweet music (the lords, Act III, iii). Caliban, who is used to the sounds, describes them as:-

> *Cal.* ...noises, sounds and sweet airs, that give delight,
> and hurt not.
> Sometimes a thousand twanging instruments
> Will hum about mine ears; and sometimes voices,
> That, if I had wak'd after long sleep,
> Will make me sleep again...[9]

The hum is associated with the sound of bees:-

> *Ariel.* [Song] Where the bee sucks there suck I:
> In a cowslip's bell I lie...[10]

Bees are an ages-old symbol for all initiates employed in

the service of God, organised into hives or lodges, who vibrate with the sound of the creative Word, *HUM* (or *AUM*). The sound of life that underlies the universe, and which some mystics or yogis are able to hear, is described as a 'hum', and this sound is associated with the vibrant Æther or Holy Spirit.

Notably, it is 'some heavenly music' which completes Prospero's spell, when he has abjured his rough magic and immediately before he breaks his staff and drowns his book in the act of mercy, the higher magic:-

> *Pros.*   But this rough magic
> I here abjure; and, when I have requir'd
> Some heavenly music,—which even now I do,—
> To work mine end upon their senses, that
> This airy charm is for, I'll break my staff,
> Bury it certain fadoms in the earth,
> And deeper than did ever plummet sound
> I'll drown my book.[11]

Prospero's staff is emblematic of the spiritual *Fire*, whilst the book signifies spiritual *Water*, but these are the earthy representations of that heavenly wisdom and intelligence, and their powers. Prospero no longer needs them when he has released the truer, higher version, although he did need them to get to that high point of self-knowledge and surrender.

Kundalini

Prospero first released Ariel from the trunk of a pine tree. The pine is a synonym for the spine of man, in which is the narrow channel known as the sixth ventricle (the cleft), known in Eastern Tantric teachings as the *sushumna*. It is up this channel that the *kundalini* rises. *Kundalini* is a Tantric term for the mercurial firewater which is said to be stored at the base of the spine and which will, when the person is in a sufficient state of purity and love, rise up the spine. Kundalini is symbolised as a serpent, the *shakti* (goddess) of Shiva. Western tradition knows this as the serpent or dragon (*i.e.* the serpent energy or dragon energy). This energy is associated with our psychic power and intelligence.

In the evolution of the human soul this serpent energy is made to rise up the spine from the base, like sap rises up a tree, building and developing the psychic body and its chakras, increasing our consciousness and intelligence, until it can be released from the crown of the head in a burst of illumination, as a fountain of energy, a fountain of life.

Symbolising this is Mercury's wand, the thyrsus, which is tipped at both top and bottom with a pinecone, representing the spine of man with the pineal gland at the top and the sacrum-coccyx at the base. Mercury's other wand, the caduceus, has the same significance, but shows the rising serpent energy in its triple-aspected form (*i.e.* solar, lunar and mercurial) rising up the spine as two serpents spiralling around the shaft and with the third serpent represented by the central shaft. The golden globe and eagle's wings at the head of the caduceus represent the illumination of the mind produced by the arisen serpent energy.

Ariel can thus be seen to be this kundalini energy, released from the base of the spine by Prospero and made to rise through all the chakras of his being, progressively raising and increasing his consciousness and power, until it reaches his crown and can be fully released in a blaze of light, a consummation of love.

The progressive raising and releasing of this energy is represented by the symbols associated with the zodiacal sign of Scorpio. From the earthiness of the scorpion the energy rises as a serpent until it takes flight as the eagle, soaring to the heights and bestowing clairvoyance (*i.e.* clear sight or perception) and the power to command angels, both of which Prospero has. The crowning culmination, however, is the stage where the eagle becomes the dove, descending again in humility and love to bless the world and thereby bringing peace.

Sacred tradition notes that angels, like human souls, evolve. The 'fallen' angel that is the spirit of man is embodied in and as the soul of man, and evolves as the human soul, which is a form of intelligence. This intelligence is associated with the kundalini energy—the serpent energy. Venus, who is associated with Ariel (see above), is sometimes symbolised as a serpent, for the spirit of love and goodwill is the real intelligence and life force contained within us, which in Rosicrucian teachings has to be discovered 'naked'. Jupiter's symbol, however, is an eagle. Jupiter's angelic equivalent is Zadkiel, Ariel's higher counterpart into which Ariel can evolve: hence the serpent can become the eagle. Zadkiel's, or Jupiter's, higher counterpart is Divine Love, represented by the dove.

In the play, Ariel's plea for freedom, as well as his plea for Prospero to show mercy, would appear to be Ariel's desire to become part of Jupiter's sphere; that is to say, to be released from being just Ariel so as to become Zadkiel, the spirit of Mercy. This is done, and can only be done, through the action of Prospero, whose spirit Ariel is.

Easter Chick

Prospero calls Ariel 'my bird' (IV, i, 185) and 'chick' (V, i, 316). This can well refer to the eagle and dove imagery, as well as to that of robin and sparrow mentioned earlier (see Chapter 3). But, besides this, the 'chick' imagery conjures up the idea of the Easter chick hatching from its egg, which symbolism is also highly appropriate to the meaning of the story.

The Easter chick is an emblem of the Son of God (*i.e.* the Word of God, also known as Mercury)[12] incarnate in the psyche of man. The egg itself is an excellent symbol of the egg-shaped psychic body and aura of a person, from which the mercurial spirit of love emerges when the time is right and the person has made the requisite effort and self-sacrifice. The psyche is the natural soul, whilst the mercurial spirit, born from the psyche, is the spiritual soul, described in alchemical texts as a golden sun (*i.e.* sol/soul) arising from the horizon of our earth or natural self.

Robin Goodfellow

Ariel can also be described as a Puck or Robin Goodfellow, which is particularly apparent in his ditty: 'Where the bee sucks, there suck I...' Robin is the name of the good person or good fellow who gives his/her life for the good of everyone else. The bird by this name has its name because of its red breast, symbolic of the love poured out from the heart of the good person. It is this 'red rose' of love, blooming on the breast, which is a sign of the true soul. Symbolically the robin is akin to the phoenix, which is a dove with a purple-red breast, meaning the same as the red-breasted robin. In the banquet scene, in a sudden ecstasy, Sebastian homes in on this truth:-

> *Seb.* ...Now I will believe
> That there are unicorns; that in Arabia
> There is one tree, the phoenix' throne; one phoenix
> At this hour reigning there.[13]

Archetypal Form

Ariel works for Prospero when Prospero gives the right commands, which issue from a good ethical motivation and are directed by a reasonably clear vision of what is going on. All this constitutes Prospero's 'best pleasure'—his Art—which Ariel serves and of which Ariel is the spiritual embodiment or 'idea'. Such living ideas or intelligencies are equated with angels (*ang-el* means 'idea of God') in the Hebraic-Christian tradition, and were referred to by Plato and Bacon as 'Forms', being the archetypal ideas or spiritual forms that embody the laws of nature and the universe. As Bacon wrote:-

> The true Natural Magic…is that great liberty and latitude of operation which dependeth upon the knowledge of Forms.[14]

> But whosover knoweth any Form, knoweth the utmost possibility of super-inducing that nature upon any variety of matter…[15]

Ariel can thus be seen to be a particular 'Form' that Prospero is becoming increasingly conversant with during the course of the play.

Service

Ariel, as a spirit of love, is *a priori* a spirit of service, for service is the fulfilment of the nature of love. Hence Ariel is described during the course of the play as a fine, dainty, diligent and industrious servant. Since Ariel serves Prospero, whose name means 'to bring pleasure', Ariel actually serves Prospero's 'best pleasure': for Prospero's best pleasure is, of course, that which is the best to bring pleasure—*i.e.* the most noble, edifying, loving and wise.

> *Ariel.*   All hail, great master! grave sir, hail! I come
> To answer thy best pleasure; be't to fly,
> To swim, to dive into the fire, to ride
> On the curl'd clouds; to thy strong bidding task
> Ariel and all his quality.[16]

Ariel is the perfect servant, for service or charity is the primary virtue of love. But the spirit of love is not something to be owned; indeed, it cannot be owned, but only set free from within ourselves. This is the lesson that the human soul has to learn, the ultimate stage of which is to release the spirit of love to such a degree that it becomes totally unlimited, free even of an adept's own personal wishes.

The full and unconditional release of love is the final stage that makes a master, which goes hand in hand with the complete and absolute surrender of the will of the human soul and personality to the universal and largely unknown will of God. It means trusting totally in the power of love alone, and offering oneself in service to something vastly greater that is beyond human comprehension. This is the ultimate sacrifice and glory of the human soul, which is not made out of weakness or feebleness, but from a position of great strength and ability. Perhaps Shakespeare had in mind here the supreme sacrifice made by the Lord Jesus Christ, who was a pattern for the rest of us.

Servant & Master

The startling truth is that the greatest lord or master is at the same time the humblest servant. It is the lordship or mastership in Prospero that Ariel encourages Prospero more and more to set free, which is none other than Ariel himself. Ariel, whilst serving Prospero's 'best pleasure', at the same time acts as the hierophant for Prospero's own development.

> *Ariel.*   Let me remember thee what thou hast promis'd,
>   Which is not yet perform'd me.
> *Pros.*   How now? moody?
>   What is't thou canst demand?
> *Ariel.*   My liberty.[17]

Ariel

Ariel.   Remember I have done thee worthy service,
Told thee no lies, made thee no mistakings, serv'd
Without or grudge, or grumblings; thou did promise
To bate me a full year.[18]

Ariel.   Do you love me, master? no?
Pros.   Dearly, my delicate Ariel.[19]

Ariel.   On the sixth hour; at which time, my Lord
You said our work should cease.
Pros.   I did say so,
When first I raised the tempest. [20]

Ariel.   Your charm so strongly works 'em
That if you now beheld them, your affections
Would become tender.
Pros.   Dost thou think so, spirit?
Ariel.   Mine would, Sir, were I human.
Pros.   And mine shall.[21]

Ariel.   Was't well done?
Pros.   Bravely, my diligence. Thou shalt be free.[22]

5. Plots & Themes

The Main Plot

The main plot of *The Tempest* is quite clearly the story of Prospero as magus or magician on his island and how, at an auspicious moment in time, he deals with the people who have wronged him. Outwardly it is a story of magic, although essentially it is one of judgement, justice, forgiveness and mercy, and the operations of a natural science in ways that we would call magical. In fact magic was once the proper name for the operations of a science based on knowledge of metaphysical laws rather than just physical laws, although nowadays we tend to abuse the name by referring to magic disparagingly as either a trick or else something produced by a science we don't ourselves understand. Bacon, for instance, described 'the true natural magic' as 'that great liberty and latitude of operation which dependeth upon the knowledge of Forms [*i.e.* Spirits or Intelligencies, which are the metaphysical Laws]'.[1] Metaphysical laws are essentially moral laws, the highest of which is divine love. The lesser laws or spirits, including physical laws, are controlled by the higher ones.

The primary 'Form' or Intelligence that Prospero works with is personified by Ariel, the spirit of compassion. Since the traditional view of 'Man' is that we are each a microcosm of the macrocosm, and therefore all divinity and spirituality lies hidden, latent within us, awaiting discovery and release, so the great spirits or archangels such as Ariel lie within us, waiting to be set free. Therefore, during the play Prospero increasingly gets to understand, know and release from himself this great spirit of love by means of a series of 'experiments'. His guinea pigs in these experiments are the king and his party. His reason for using and experimenting with this law (Ariel) is ostensibly to right wrongs and to bring about a state of affairs better than it was before.

Prospero's magic, which Shakespeare seems to have based upon stories of initiation from the ancient Mysteries, begins with a tempest and a shipwreck, which he causes, and culminates with the marriage of his daughter to the King of Naples' son, plus the restoration of his own dukedom, which is what he hoped for. In the course of this, all persons travelling on the king's ship are preserved alive, safe and unharmed, including the ship and its crew. The king's party are carefully dispersed about the island in three groups (the lords, the servants, and Ferdinand on his own), and they each go through experiences suited to their moral state. Ferdinand is brought directly to the heart of the island, Prospero's cell, and to Miranda, Prospero's 'heart', where the couple fall in love and, after being suitably tested, are given Prospero's blessing to marry. The others, less innocent, are taken through purgatorial and purification experiences, during which Prospero, with the help of Ariel, prevents the murder of Alonso by Sebastian and Antonio, and his own murder and the rape of Miranda by Caliban, Stephano and Trinculo.

Eventually, after their cathartic experiences, the lords are brought to the heart of the island and, in a magic circle before Prospero's cell, they are forgiven by Prospero, released from the magic spell and given their freedom. Friendships are made and Prospero's dukedom is restored to him. Finally, the lovers are revealed and Ferdinand is restored to his father, the king, who now gains a daughter. Caliban and the other two servants are admonished but forgiven, and, as in *The Merchant of Venice*, the ship, which was thought lost, is found to be safe and in better shape than before, complete with its crew and ready to sail. With all brought to a happy fruition and the sinners redeemed, Ariel is set free and Prospero turns to us, the audience, to likewise set him free.

In all this Prospero presents three aspects to his character, like a trinity.

One aspect is that of a staunch defender of truth and stern judge who is concerned with righteousness and justice. The truth that he defends is personified by Miranda, Prospero's heart and life. However, he also includes in this truth the original state of affairs in which he was duke of Milan before he was deposed, into which position he was born as if by divine right. He likewise defends Alonso, the rightful king of Naples, and preserves the king's life from the would-be murderers. He also preserves his own life and Miranda's, and that of all the others: for life itself is truth. He judges the three 'men of sin' and the drunken, malicious servants, and sets out to bring them to a state of repentance by means of certain experiences that have a cathartic effect.

A second aspect is that of a loving father and compassionate ruler or 'king'. He begins as a loving father, and his severity in administering justice is tempered with mercy from the start, such as in the care he takes to preserve the lives of all concerned in order to do good. He is by no means perfect in this love, though, and he is harsh towards Ariel at the beginning, not understanding Ariel's words. However, his compassion grows, particularly when he heeds the suggestion of Ariel to be merciful, culminating in the forgiving of the sins of the 'three men of sin' once the point of repentance has been reached. In this Prospero takes on the role of a redeemer, for mercy redeems.

The third aspect that Prospero shows is that of a hierophant, who both reforms and initiates those who come into his aura and realm of responsibility. He is a teacher and a tester, an oracle, and a philosopher-scientist who knows from experience and can share that knowledge with others, revealing the truth to them.

In Cabala these three aspects relate to the trinity of Judgement, Mercy and Knowledge, symbolised respectively by Mars, Jupiter and Saturn, which themselves are reflections or emanations of the Holy Trinity of Intelligence, Wisdom and Power. All these are aspects of Divine Love, for God is Love. How to balance them in proper harmony so as to bring about a state of goodness and joy is the work of the magus. When achieved, such a magus would become a Hermes Trismegistus ('the thrice greatest'), having 'the power and fortune of a king, the knowledge and illumination of a priest, and the learning and universality of a philosopher'.[2]

The Four Sub-Plots

Within the main story or plot there are four principal sub-plots. These are:-

1. The courtship, betrothal and marriage of Ferdinand & Miranda;
2. The search for Alonso's lost son and heir, Ferdinand;
3. Antonio and Sebastian's plot to murder Alonso and his friends;
4. The servants' plot to murder Prospero and rape Miranda.

These four sub-plots make two pairs. The first two sub-plots are acts of love, although different in nature: one being a joyful experience and the other being sorrowful. Of these, the former involves discovering someone and something (a love) that was not known of before, whilst the latter involves losing someone who was known and loved. The second two sub-plots, by contrast, are acts of evil and very similar in nature, differing only in degree and clarity of consciousness, one involving conspirators who know perfectly well what they are doing, and the other involving conspirators who do not really know what they are doing. In the former instance a perfectly sober, well-educated and privileged nobleman cold-bloodedly plots to murder his brother in order to be king of Naples, urged on and assisted by another equally cultured nobleman who has already, as far as he is concerned, killed his brother, the rightful duke of Milan, and usurped his position. In the latter instance a savage, half-human, illiterate servant urges on a drunken butler and his equally drunk friend, a jester, to kill the king of the island, so that the butler (Stephano) might rule in Prospero's place and forcefully make Miranda his enslaved queen and mother of his children.

The Background Plot

Behind all this is an underlying story concerning the law of love and how it operates. This law is personified by Ariel, a spirit of mercy or compassion, who carries out the will of Prospero, howbeit with great latitude of choice as to how it should be done. This merciful love, Ariel, acts as servant to Prospero, but in fact teaches and inspires Prospero as well as being master of all the lesser spirits and elements and, seemingly, of human beings of lesser stature than Prospero. The work of this spirit moves unceasingly towards one aim—

freedom: freedom of itself from the elements and Prospero's personal will, but also freedom for Prospero and Miranda, and for the others who are trapped on the island. At the same time this spirit of mercy does not supersede the spirit of justice, but enables justice to be acted out whilst enhancing and completing it with love and joy. This background plot, therefore, is a fine illustration of the great laws of karma (justice) and redemption (mercy), the latter law being greater than the former, but operating without in any way taking away the former.

This story can even be understood, and perhaps is intended to be understood, on a greater scale, as an allegory of the fall of mankind and his redemption: for Prospero falls from his original blessed position as duke of Milan as a result of his unbalanced, obsessive desire for knowledge. Such an inordinate and selfish thirst for knowledge, at the expense of looking after his paradisiacal kingdom, is said to have caused the fall of Adam and his partner Eve from Eden. Yet, at the same time mankind is intended to learn and to have knowledge of God, of Truth. This intention is said to be the very purpose of mankind, whose generic name (*man*) means 'mind' or 'thinker'.

> In sum, I would advise all in general, that they would take into serious consideration the true and genuine ends of knowledge; that they seek it not either for pleasure, or contention, or contempt of others, or for profit, or fame, or for honour and promotion, or such like adulterate or inferior ends; but for the merit and emolument of life; and that they regulate and perfect the same in charity. For the desire of power was the fall of angels, the desire of knowledge the fall of man; but in charity there is no excess, neither man nor angels ever incurred danger by it.[3]

From this point of view the background plot is nothing

else but a suggestion as to how paradise might be regained. Moreover the play includes the hint that is spoken of in the wisdom traditions, that the fall of man was intentionally allowed in order to bring about an even greater blessing than would have been possible if the fall had not occurred. In *The Tempest* allegory this is alluded to by Gonzalo:-

> *Gon.*   Was Milan thrust from Milan, that his issue
> Should become kings of Naples? O rejoice
> Beyond a common joy! And set it down,
> With gold on lasting pillars: in one voyage
> Did Claribel her husband find at Tunis,
> And Ferdinand, her brother, found a wife
> Where he himself was lost, Prospero his dukedom
> In a poor isle, and all of us ourselves
> When no man was his own.[4]

Joy is said to be the ultimate blessing—not a common joy, but the ecstatic one of knowing truth, knowing God, knowing oneself, knowing one's other self, knowing love. That which was lost is found! It is in the losing and finding that we get to know it. The lasting pillars are the Twin Pillars or Pillars of Solomon, the immovable Cabalistic and Freemasonic landmarks on which are inscribed in alchemical gold the words of truth—the truth of being and the truth of knowing.[5]

Themes

Magic

The major theme of *The Tempest* is almost certainly magic, with which, by means of thought, Prospero conjures up a spirit called Ariel and commands him to carry out various tasks:-

Pros. Come with a thought. I thank thee. Ariel: come.
Ariel. Thy thoughts I cleave to.[6]

Ariel's tasks range from the manipulation of the physical laws and elements to produce various phenomena at will, such as the tempest, water that does not wet, fire that does not burn, wind, fine weather, thunder and lightning, to a control over metaphysical laws (spirits) and elements that induce drowsiness or other atmospheric moods, and produce dreams, visions and apparitions of various kinds. In addition Ariel has magic of his own, beyond Prospero's control, including the sounds that he makes, whether of roaring beasts or sweet music, or the hum of bees or voices, with the associated ability to attract or repel, and to inspire fear, terror, harmony or love.

This magic, which is carried out in partnership between Prospero and Ariel, is however good magic. It is inspired with good motives and intended for increasingly philanthropic purposes. It is what great Renaissance philosophers such as Henry Cornelius Agrippa and Giordano Bruno referred to as high intellectual and virtuous magic, in which a pure intellect is conjoined with the powers of the gods,[7] rather than the debased witchcraft and sorcery associated with the evil witch Sycorax and her dark god Setebos. The one is 'white' magic and the other is 'black' magic.

To help make this contrast, Shakespeare has used the Cabalistic symbolism of the Twin Pillars, also known as the Great Pillars, or Pillars of Solomon, or Pillars of Hercules. Sycorax's magic is associated with the moon and tides, whilst Prospero's magic is associated with Ariel. In Cabala, the moon is used as a symbol of the left-hand 'dark' pillar of the cabalistic Tree of Life, whilst the sun is the corresponding symbol for the 'light' right-hand pillar. These two pillars, which are represented graphically in the Tree of Life diagram and architecturally at the entrance to Solomon's Temple, represent all the polarities of life and the universe, from light and dark in the wholly good sense to light and dark in the sense of good and evil. At one level of interpretation the left-hand pillar is associated with divine intelligence, the reflective mind of God, whilst the right-hand pillar is associated with divine wisdom, the radiant heart of God. At another level of interpretation the left-hand pillar signifies the psyche (the natural soul), whose focus is in the head, whilst the right-hand pillar signifies the spiritual soul, whose focus is in the heart. Ariel, as the archangel of compassion or mercy, belongs to the right-hand solar pillar of the Tree of Life. His counterpart, signifying judgement or severity on the left-hand lunar pillar, is the archangel Samael. Samael is said to have a dark or evil aspect, whose intention is to oppose and destroy all good things. Setebos would seem to be the Patagonian equivalent of Samael.

Prospero's magic is an art—one could say, *the* Art—that is concerned with the mastery and control of nature. But nature includes man himself: so Prospero is as concerned with mastering his own passions, to make them good, as in mastering the elements:-

> *Pros.*   Though with their high wrongs I am struck to th'
>   quick,
>   Yet with my nobler reason 'gainst my fury
>   Do I take part: the rarer action is
>   In virtue than in vengeance...[8]

Likewise he is properly concerned with improving his art, as his knowledge and experience increases. So, learning from his experience and from Ariel, he abjures his rough magic for an even better art:-

> *Pros.*...But this rough magic,
>   I here abjure; and when I have requir'd
>   Some heavenly music,—which even now I do...[9]

The heavenly music is representative of the higher, better art, as allegorised in the story of the Thracian poet-musician Orpheus, or of Apollo with his lyre. Heavenly music is of the heart, being the harmonious sound of love, the divine Word.[10]

Science

Directly associated with this art or magic is the idea of Prospero as a scientist and moral reformer. In fact, in Shakespeare's time the term 'science', as defined and promoted so passionately by Bacon, included a working knowledge of both physics and metaphysics. That is to say, complete science was seen to embrace a science of the soul as well as a science of the physical universe, plus a science of the spirit—the realm of gods, angels and archetypes. In terms of human beings, soul matters are concerned *a priori* with morals—the domain of thoughts, emotions and psychological behaviour. Emotion governs thought, and thought governs behaviour. These psychological or moral matters then in turn govern physical matter, manifesting themselves outwardly in the natural, corporeal world. The spiritual world has the power to govern the psychological world, but, in terms of respecting human freewill, it does so only when invoked or asked to help: for essentially the spiritual world is one of pure love, and the nature of love is to inspire and serve. 'Ask, and you shall receive,'[11] is a key teaching, but always bearing in mind that the good spirits, like Ariel, only respond to good requests. To make one's will God's will is the corresponding key teaching. Prayer is a science—a science based on love.

In other words a true scientist (as defined by Bacon, Agrippa and others, and portrayed by Shakespeare in Prospero) is a virtuous and philanthropic magician or 'magus', knowledgeable and proficient in the three worlds of body, soul and spirit, and inspired by love (God).

> For certain it is that God worketh nothing in nature but by second causes… But farther, it is an assured truth, and a conclusion of experience, that a little or superficial knowledge of Philosophy may incline the mind of man towards Atheism, but a farther proceeding therein doth bring the mind back again to Religion: for in the entrance of philosophy, when the second causes, which are next the senses, do offer themselves unto the mind of man, if it swell and stay there it may induce some oblivion of the highest cause; but when a man passeth on further, and seeth the dependence of causes, and the works of Providence, then, according to the allegory of the poets, he will easily believe that the highest link of Nature's chain must needs be tied at the foot of Jupiter's chair.[12]

Jupiter's chair is the realm of Ariel—the spirit of compassion and mercy.

Prospero's science includes Cabalistic, Hermetic, Neoplatonic and Christian knowledge, in synthesis. As a character he may well be partly modelled on the Elizabethan mage, Dr John Dee, who died in 1608,[13] but also on many earlier magi. It should also be noted that Prospero is a pointer towards a self-portrait of the author Shakespeare, who knows, uses and teaches the higher sciences in his great Art. The obvious ideal, though, that Prospero (Shakespeare) is aiming for, is that of Jesus Christ, who demonstrated a complete command over nature, raising and stilling storms, feeding the thousands, inspiring dreams and visions, healing the sick, raising the dead to life, teaching both publicly and privately, rebuking both his disciples and the Pharisees when necessary, chasing corrupt moneychangers and merchants out of the temple, bestowing justice with mercy, forgiving and loving all—and, at the end of his public ministry, giving up all his magic and throwing himself on the mercy of his audience. Because of the ignorance of those he appealed to, Jesus was crucified. ('Father, forgive them, for they know not what they do.')[14]

All in all, Prospero is a portrayal of the ideal of the Rosicrucian philosopher-scientist—someone who can, as Jesus himself pointed out, do as Jesus did and more.[15] In Prospero the author presents a vision of a humanity who are not ignorant, not corrupt, and who consciously, deliberately and scientifically develop the art of righting wrongs, bestowing mercy and creating a better world based on love.

Justice & Mercy

Justice and mercy constitute another theme running through the play, as in virtually all the Shakespeare plays. Justice is equated with judgement and severity, and also with karma, harshly defined in the Bible as an eye for an eye, a tooth for a tooth, a life for a life…[16] Justice is the universal law of compensation. It needs mercy to balance and mitigate its severity. Mercy is equated with compassion and forgiveness, which adds opportunity to the karmic compensation, and can creatively transmute any situation to a higher and better state of affairs. Mercy is the universal law of redemption, which is known as the higher of the two laws.

In human evolution we tend to develop the severe, righteous, karmic side first, before we learn how to use mercy. Cabalistically justice is represented by Mars, the strict warrior, whilst mercy is signified by Jupiter, the generous king. The king is greater and more powerful than the warrior, but evolution takes us through the warrior stage before we enter the sovereignty stage—a path of progress that is reflected in the initiations taught in the Mystery schools. First comes discipleship, in which we purify and discipline ourselves. Then comes adepthood, in which we can enlighten others and do truly good work. The first stage is represented by baptism by water, the second by baptism by fire and holy breath (holy spirit).[17]

Prospero epitomises this path of development, beginning with a nature far more severe than merciful towards his perceived enemies. But he is not unloving, nor uncaring. Unlike Hamlet, for instance, he wishes harm to no one, and his merciful nature is gradually awakened into its full powers, especially at the critical juncture when Ariel suggests that his affections should become tender towards the three men of sin and their companions (v, i, 17-19). This crisis should not be missed, for it comes at the point, and only at the point, when Alonso, Sebastian and Antonio have become repentant. That is to say, mercy can only be creatively given when it is genuinely asked for or needed, and a contrite heart needs to form part of the request:-

> *Pros.*...they being penitent,
> The sole drift of my purpose doth extend not a frown further.[18]

Besides the qualities of mercy and justice being developed and acted out in the person of Prospero, their archetypes are also personified in the characters of Miranda and Ferdinand. Miranda shows her compassion right at the start of the play, when her heart cries out for the people caught in the shipwreck, and then later for Ferdinand when he is put to work in chains by Prospero. Ferdinand, however, is a staunch warrior and perfectly capable of not only swimming bravely to shore but of subjecting himself to the harsh discipline which Prospero imposes on him.

Both Miranda and Ferdinand are loving, even though they each represent the opposite polarities of mercy and justice: and this is a key. God is love,[19] and both justice and mercy are aspects of love; but these two aspects, although polar opposites, need to manifest together. Each is not complete without the other. The betrothal and marriage of Miranda and Ferdinand symbolise this. Their union represents the Mystical Marriage—the marriage of opposites in love that brings harmony and beauty. Beauty (whether it be beauty of character, beauty of nature, beauty of sound and form, beauty of music and proportion) is the 'face of God', in which truth can be seen.[20] Herein lies the great secret of the revelation at the end—of Miranda and Ferdinand playing chess in Prospero's cell. It represents the moment in the Mysteries when the veil is removed, revealing the truth concealed in the inner chamber, the chamber of the heart. Such a revelation of beauty is joy.

> *Gon.* ...O rejoice
> Beyond a common joy!... [21]

Freedom and Joy

Joy and freedom are inextricably linked. Freedom, true freedom, brings joy.

Throughout the play both imprisonment and freedom constitute a regular, on-going theme. Prospero and Miranda are prisoners on the island, cut off from their roots—their home, family, friends and dukedom. Alonso and his party are prisoners on the island through Prospero's magic. Ariel, although set free from the pine and Sycorax's curse, still remains a partial prisoner of Prospero. Caliban, because of his dangerous lust and attempted violence against Miranda, is a slave of Prospero and Miranda, and later puts himself in voluntary thrall to the drunkards, Stephano and Trinculo. They all (with the exception perhaps of Miranda, who has known nothing else) want freedom from their respective imprisonments.

In addition, they are each in various states of moral imprisonment and karmic debt. Prospero is perhaps the only one who recognises this and tries to do something about it, which indeed is an adept's duty. Through his magic and his own personal development, he helps all the characters to find some level of freedom from their moral chains and karma, whether they be guilts or vices, evils of one sort or another, or simply lack of suitable experience, or parental and filial duties, or unfulfilled love.

Just as there are various levels of human development and morality, so there are various degrees of freedom. Each evolutionary movement from one level to a higher one is a freedom, and each freedom brings an experience of joy. But only the final freedom from the penultimate level releases us into the state of joy unlimited and unending. Shakespeare shows us the various major levels of human development in the characters of *The Tempest,* ranging from brute to enlightened soul. He also shows how joy is experienced at the end by all, but in varying degrees, depending on what degree of freedom has been achieved.

Freedom essentially refers to a 'state of love', since the word is derived from the Sanskrit root, *pri*, meaning love. Ariel, besides being an angel, epitomises the love that infuses this freedom, but it requires the will and behaviour of the human being to effect it. That is to say, by releasing love from ourselves, we release ourselves.

Swami Sri Yukteswar, in his book *The Holy Science*, explains the concept of freedom and joy very succinctly, in terms of both Eastern and Western wisdom traditions. For instance, Parabrahma (God) is one, indivisible Being—everlasting, complete, without beginning or end. But Parabrahma has two aspects, of which It is the origin: (1) power which is joy, and (2) knowledge which is love, thereby being what Western tradition refers to as the Holy Trinity:-

> Parabrahma (God) is everlasting, complete, without
> beginning or end. It is one indivisible Being. In It is the ori-
> gin of all knowledge and love, the root of all power and
> joy.[22]

Cabala refers to the power and joy as Divine Wisdom (*i.e.* the Word), and to the knowledge and love as the Holy Intelligence (*i.e.* the Holy Ghost or Spirit). As Sri Yukteswar explains, the Eternal Joy (*Ananda*) is the Almighty Force (*Shakti*) that produces the world; whilst the divine knowledge and love is the Omniscient Feeling (*Chit*) that makes this world conscious and demonstrates the Nature (*Prakriti*) of God.

From the point of view that God is Love, joy is the radiance of that love which creates through its power—a power that sets up vibration (its sound or music) in its intelligent, receptive polarity. It is the Word of God, 'lost' (to us) in the cosmos that it creates within the divine Intelligence, so that we can find it and know it. When Gonzalo exclaims 'joy!' he is referring in fact to what is known in Freemasonry as the Lost Word, which he has now found. Alonso follows this exclamation with a prayer, a wish to give joy to Miranda and Ferdinand, to bless their marriage. Gonzalo properly completes this prayer with the 'Amen', which has the meaning of 'So be it' and which is the mantric sound of the Word as used in the Christian tradition, equivalent to the *Aum* of Hinduism and Buddhism.

> *Gon.* …O rejoice
>   Beyond a common joy!…
> *Alon.*   Give me your hands:
>   Let grief and sorrow still embrace his heart
>   That doth not wish you joy!
> *Gon.*   Be it so! Amen! [23]

The omniscient feeling, the 'all knowledge and love',

refers to the receptive, reflective, responsive aspect of divine love—the intelligence that is conscious of all, loves all, understands all and knows all. Such omniscient feeling or love is pure enjoyment of joy. Gonzalo refers to this in his exclamation, 'O rejoice…!' Rejoicing is the enjoyment of joy. It is what is called ecstasy, the bliss state, or illumination: for joy is a 'sun' that illuminates, and rejoicing is the state of being illuminated (*i.e.* illumination). When we have joy, we shine.

In union there is no difference: love is joy, joy is love. This is God. Occasionally we reach such union, called *yoga* in the East. A perfect master is in that union all the time. He is totally free (*Sannyasi*).

> And then he saw that Brahman was joy;
> And from joy all beings have come,
> By joy they all live,
> And unto joy they all return.[24]

6. The Four Levels of Human Evolution

Out of all the Shakespeare plays *The Tempest* is remarkable in
depicting virtually the whole spectrum of human development in an archetypal way, from human grossness to the
exaltation of the human spirit. Moreover it does this by using
allegorical tests and imagery equivalent to those of the
ancient Mystery schools, coupling this with some of the symbolism used in Freemasonry which was then beginning to
emerge in its modern speculative form. The play is designed
on a framework that depicts what the Hermetic philosophers
knew as the four main levels of human evolution, each level
being represented by a major life cycle of a particular type
and quality, and each cycle having four main stages of development.

The Four Stages of the Life Cycle

In the language of Alchemy the four basic stages of every life
cycle are symbolised by the four alchemical elements, *earth-
water-air-fire*, depicting how life transforms itself in both
nature and mankind with the eventual aim of manifesting
light (*æther*), the quintessence. The burning candle is a good
example of this process and alchemical symbolism. The candle wax transforms from solid (*earth*) to liquid (*water*) to
vapour (*air*) to flame (*fire*), and then becomes a blazing 'sun'
of light (*æther*) within the flame and shining from the flame.
The changes from solid to liquid to vapour to flame are all

transformations, but the change from flame to light is a transmutation: the former changes are all within a limited sphere of expression, whilst the change from flame to light leaps beyond those initial boundaries, with light becoming relatively free or unlimited (*i.e.* light shines far beyond the flame and the other limiting forms of the candle). Moreover, the nature of light is different to that of a candle in all its forms, and has the power, in its heat, to keep the candle burning.

However, not everything necessarily transmutes. Instead of a transmutation at the end of a cycle of transformation there can be a recycling. For instance, in terms of

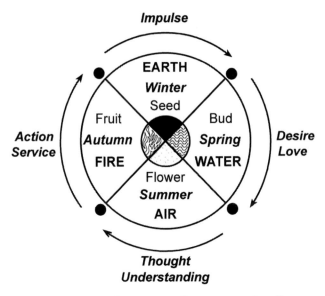

3. The Alchemical Cycle of the Seasons and Life Process

An impulse (internal or external) gives rise to a desire or wish, leading to a thought about how to fulfil that desire, then an action which fulfils the desire as far as possible. Knowledge is derived from the result of the action, which we can choose to learn from or not.

nature and the natural process that goes on during an annual cycle of time, we can recognise the four seasons of winter, spring, summer and autumn, and what they each produce. In the winter (*earth*) the seed lies in the ground and the sap is fallen in the trees and plants. In the spring (*water*) the sap rises and green buds and shoots burst forth into the light of day. In the summer (*air*) the plants and trees spread their leaves wide open and blossom into flower. In the autumn (*fire*) their fruit is produced. In the fruit is the seed of a new cycle of life. But, in order for this new cycle of life to take place, the fruit has to die, just as the year dies, so as to release its seed into the ground for yet more expression of life.

In this cycle of the seasons there is no transmutation, although there can be increasing abundance, since one good seed can produce a plant with many seeds in its fruit, or many fruits with seed, or both. But if, say, the seed produced by the plant was wheat grain, we could make that grain into bread and eat it. By means of that act the nature of the plant would be transmuted into the nature of our human body, which is a higher and less limited state of existence.

In allegorical stories, such as those of Shakespeare, natural symbols of the seasons, besides the seasons themselves, are used to denote these four stages of the life process: such as rocks, seed, snow, ice, coldness, darkness, wildness, storms, night, for the stage of *earth*; water, springs, buds, dawn, springtime flowers, for the stage of *water*; flowers generally, trees, air, perfume, incense, full daylight, for the stage of *air*; and fire, fruit, food, harvest, sunset, for the stage of *fire*.

The life process, however, does not just occur in nature, as physical or physiological processes, it also operates in the psychological and spiritual realms of existence. For instance, as human beings we go through cycles of birth, growth, maturity and decay (death)—not just in terms of an individual life span but also in terms of smaller life cycles within that whole life span. In psychological rather than physical/physiological matters the fundamental cycle of human life, in terms of how we live life, can be expressed as an impulse (*earth*) followed by a desire (*water*) followed by a thought (*air*) followed by an action (*fire*), repeated over and over again.

After each action has finished we can gain a little knowledge from the experience, which can assist us in our next impulse and cycle. In this way we can, with consistent effort and self-education, gradually better ourselves, raising our desires to a level of love, our thoughts to a level of understanding, and our actions to become useful and of service to all life. This is what is called the path of initiation, and by this means we become noble or holy. The development of this nobleness or holiness of character also brings illumination: for love is light, and experiential knowledge of love, as put into action with understanding, is illumination.

The Druids referred to the path of initiation as learning to love truth, learning to understand truth and learning to serve truth, which three are the foundations of *Awen* (*i.e.* holiness, illumination). Christianity (in the words of St Paul)[1] names these three stages which result from the initial impulse as faith, hope and charity: faith in God, which is our fundamental willingness to trust in love and goodwill; hope, which is our vision and understanding of that love; and charity, which is living a life of love and understanding put into practice as goodness and service. Charity is called the greatest of the three because it fulfils the three: it is the fruit of the cycle.

The sages throughout all time have known this truth. It has formed the fundamental teaching of the many Mystery schools scattered throughout the world in all ages, and underlies the great religions that are an exoteric expression of the Mysteries for the general public. The three stages of love, understanding and service, which develop from an initial impulse, constitute the basis of all initiation, all human training and development, ascending by degrees to the glory of masterhood.

The Four Cycles of Human Evolution

Just as there are the four fundamental stages to each cycle of life, so there are four basic cycles, each one leading to the next, and with each successive cycle being more highly evolved than the previous one. In Alchemy these four basic cycles are known respectively as (1) Preparation, (2) the Lesser Work, (3) the Greater Work and (4) the After Work. They are represented by the four alchemical elements—*viz.* Preparation (*Earth*), Lesser Work (*Water*), Greater Work (*Air*), and After Work (*Fire*). As implied by the symbolism of the alchemical elements, there is a correlation between these four cycles and the four stages of each individual cycle.

The first of these cycles is gross, the second is ordinary, the third is virtuous, and the fourth is exalted. They are associated respectively with the processes of purgation, purification, refinement and sublimation. When human beings reach the third cycle, they enter the path of initiation as a disciple, which culminates in full initiateship. The fourth cycle is that of the adept, which culminates in full mastery—the perfect expression of divine love. Without the requisite effort we remain at the same level and experience the same type of cycle, in cycle after cycle. To move from one type or level of cycle up to a higher one involves not just a transformation but also a transmutation of the personality. Plutarch put it succinctly when he said that the souls of men pass, by a natural and divine order, from mortal men to heroes, from heroes to daemons, and finally, if completely purified and consecrated, from daemons to gods.[2]

However, it is possible for part of our psyche to be going through mundane cycles whilst at the same time another part is striving with the Lesser Mysteries and a third, more refined part is enjoying the Greater Mysteries. The burning candle is an example of this. Not only does the whole candle not turn into flame at once, but also the lower levels feed the higher. In this is a secret of life which Prospero fully grasps at the end of the play when he acknowledges Caliban as part of him:-

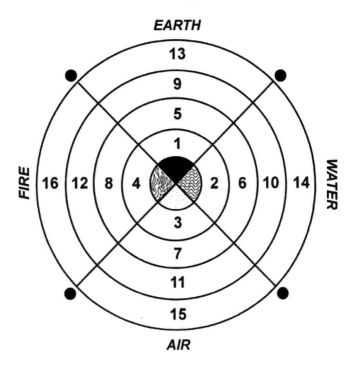

4. The Four Major Alchemical Cycles of Evolution

Gross Cycle (Earth): Stages 1-4.
Mundane Cycle (Water): Stages 5-8.
Virtuous Cycle (Air): Stages 9-12.
Exalted Cycle (Fire): Stages 13-16.

Pros.....this thing of darkness I
    Acknowledge mine.[3]

Who we basically 'are' as a person depends on where our consciousness habitually resides and how much of our psyche we have transmuted. The consciousness of an adept, for instance, will reside primarily in the exalted cycles. At the same time he or she will be aware of the other parts of the person that are still unperfected, and will be constantly working to transmute those parts, like a burning candle, until all is resolved into the light of love.

If one takes the play from the point of view of it representing one person, Prospero, with all the other characters being different parts or sub-personalities of him, then the play can be seen to be a portrayal of how one person, an adept, is trying to perfect himself, and is learning and adapting as he goes along. It may even be the author's own inner life story, told allegorically for the educational benefit of others—for certainly the author must have experienced these things in order to tell the tale so well.

In the Mystery schools the virtuous cycle of learning to love, understand and serve constituted what were known as the Lesser Mysteries of initiation. The culmination of this is illumination, which then expands and develops into a complete cycle of its own, known as the Greater Mysteries—the exalted cycle.[4]

The Four Groups of Characters

In order to show all four alchemical cycles, Shakespeare shows the life, behaviour and experiences on the island of four different groups of characters: (1) the servants; (2) the lords; (3) the lovers, Ferdinand and Miranda; and (4) the adept, Prospero. And then there is Ariel.

(1) The Servants

The king's servants, Stephano and Trinculo, together with Prospero's servant, Caliban, belong to the first 'gross' cycle, which they go through twice during the play. These three servants are gross examples of humanity—those who are sometimes termed 'less than men', who have neither the cultural qualities derived from good education nor what Ovid described as *melior natura* ('a better nature'). Of the three, Caliban might be considered an example of the semi-bestial root from which the first gross expression of humanity springs. Concerning these things, Edward Phillips and Francis Bacon had this to say:-

> [Two forces distinguish the better part of mankind from the more brutish:]…the first is that *Melior natura* which the Poet[5] speaks of, with which whoever is amply indued, take that Man from his Infancy, throw him into the Desarts of *Arabia,* there let him converse some years with Tygers and Leopards, and at last bring him where civil society and conversation abides, and ye shall see how on a sudden, the scales and dross of his barbarity purging off by degrees, he will start up a Prince or Legislator, or some such illustrious Person: the other is that noble thing call'd *Education,* this is, that Harp of *Orpheus,* that lute of *Amphion,* so elegantly figur'd by the Poets to have wrought such Miracles among irrational and insensible Creatures, which raiseth beauty even out of deformity, order and regularity out of Chaos and confusion, and which, if thoroughly and rightly prosecuted, would be able to civilize the most savage natures, & root out barbarism and ignorance from off the face of the Earth: those who have either of these qualifications singly may justly be term'd *Men*; those who have both united in a happy conjunction, *more* than *Men*; those who have neither of them in any competent measure…*less* than *Men*…[6]

They that deny a God destroy man's nobility, for certainly man is of kin to the beasts by his body, and if he be not of kin to God by his spirit, he is a base and ignoble creature. It destroys likewise magnanimity, and the raising of human nature. For take an example of a dog, and mark what a generosity and courage he will put on when he finds himself maintained by a man, who to him is in stead of a god, or *melior natura*; which courage is manifestly such as that creature, without that confidence of a better nature than his own, could never attain. So man, when he resteth and assureth himself upon divine protection and favour, gathereth a force and faith which human nature in itself could not obtain.[7]

However, through their experiences in the gross cycle on the island, repeated twice, the three servants are brought to the point where they could, with a little effort, enter the next higher cycle of ordinary humanity.

(2) The Lords

The lords naturally belong to the second cycle—that of the ordinary level of humanity, having either *melior natura* or education, or a mixture of both in some measure. However, the lords are split into two cliques, each clique experiencing the island differently according to the state of their hearts.

Alonso, Sebastian and Antonio form one clique, who see the island as a stinking marsh and desert, unsustainable of life. They are despondent, react gloomily, even spitefully, to their good fortune at being preserved alive and unharmed out of the shipwreck. In their self-centredness they can see neither the beauty of the island nor the fortune that has kept them remarkably safe. Instead of giving thanks they give curses, and make cheap mockery of those who try to help and cheer them. They each hold high positions in society and are supposedly born of good stock, yet they have corrupted and selfish natures that drag them down to the first cycle of grossness. In their corruptness they are no better than the servants—worse, it could be said, since they have the privilege of birth and education that naturally fits them for at least the second ordinary cycle, whilst the servants have neither and cannot necessarily be expected to behave otherwise than the way they do.

But the second clique of lords—Gonzalo, Francesco and Adrian—are filled with thanks and wonder at their preservation. They see the island with different eyes. They attend upon the first three; yet have a wisdom that their rulers lack. For instance Gonzalo, trying to cheer up Alonso, remarks:–

> *Gon.* Beseech you, sir, be merry; you have cause,
> So have we all, of joy; for our escape
> Is much beyond our loss. Our hint of woe
> Is common; every day, some sailor's wife,
> The masters of some merchant, and the merchant,
> Have just our theme of woe; but for the miracle,
> I mean our preservation, few in millions
> Can speak like us: then wisely, good sir, weigh
> Our sorrow with our comfort.[8]

Adrian, like Gonzalo and Francesco, whose better heart or nature allows him to see the island with clearer vision than Alonso, Sebastian or Antonio, observes:-

> *Adr.* Though this island seem to be a desert,—
> Uninhabitable, and almost inaccessible,—
> It must needs be of subtle, tender and delicate temperance.
> The air breathes upon us here most sweetly.[9]

Gonzalo adds:-

Gon. Here is everything advantageous to life.
How lush and lusty the grass looks! How green!
But the rarity of it is,—which is indeed almost beyond credit,—that our garments, being, as they were, drenched in the sea, hold, notwithstanding, their freshness and glosses, being rather new-dyed than stained with salt water.
Methinks our garments are now as fresh as when we put them on first in Afric, at the marriage of the King's fair daughter Claribel to the King of Tunis.[10]

Here we begin to touch in on some of the mystery of their condition and of the island, perceived by Gonzalo but totally missed by Alonso, Sebastian and Antonio. Furthermore, Alonso is convinced that his son is drowned, and prefers this morbid, self-indulgent state to one of hope, despite that Francesco reports otherwise:–

Fran. Sir, he may live:
I saw him beat the surges under him,
And ride upon their backs…
… I not doubt
He came alive to land.[11]

All in all, the second clique of attendant lords has the rudiments of faith, hope and charity, which the first clique of ruling lords demonstrably lack. The island offers the same conditions to both cliques, yet the reactions and behaviour of each clique is almost entirely different. The ruling lords begin by going through the first alchemical cycle, whilst their attendants are concurrently in the second. But, when the cycle of life is repeated, the experiences of the first cycle of time on the island redeem Alonso, Sebastian and Antonio to the second alchemical cycle, in which they become increasingly and genuinely repentant. Their better natures are awakened, and their sins are somewhat purged as a result.

Thus, in the second cycle of time on the island, all the lords experience the cycle at the second alchemical level. This, in turn, brings them at the end of the play to the possibility of beginning any future cycles at the next higher level if they so wish; for the example is shown them, the means presented to them, and the love, administered through forgiveness and the offer of friendship, is given to them as a divine gift to make it possible.

(3) The Lovers

Both Ferdinand and Miranda commence their joint experiences on the island in the third alchemical cycle of life, and continue in it during the course of the play. This third cycle is that of initiation, which can only begin with a pure heart. From the pure heart can flow a pure love, which in turn enables truth to be seen.[12] This allows the mind to develop understanding, which can then be followed by wise, loving and wholesome action. Virtue and affection are the hallmarks of this cycle of initiation—the natural propensities of a pure heart, which bestow the power to see and recognise God, the All-Good, and to purify, strengthen and refine the rest of the psyche.

Both Ferdinand and Miranda have this necessary purity of the heart from the start. They are each endowed with a *melior natura* in its truest sense, and added to this they each have received a good education. Unlike the lords and servants, who are compelled to experience the island by going round it as if in a maze, Ferdinand is led straight to its centre by the music of Ariel, and the initiatory experiences of the couple take place in that centre, by the cell, in the heart of the island.

Miranda's purity is a kind of innocence, yet nevertheless she has a true purity of the heart plus a wisdom which has been developed in her with the help of (a) her father's guidance and teaching, and (b) her own observations and experience of life in the natural surroundings of the island. Her purity is as yet untested in the trials of the wider world of human society, especially in terms of her own awakening sexuality and womanhood, but Prospero sets up an initial test to suit the occasion—the trial of chastity and obedience—and hammers home the lesson. At the same time he initiates Miranda into becoming independent of him, her father, so that she can grow in her own right as a woman and with her own will, making her own choices, taking her own initiatives and eventually coming to know 'what' she is.

Ferdinand's purity, on the other hand, is worldly-wise. He has it despite the society in which he lives and out of which he has emerged. Added to this he has courage, determination, and a strong individuality and self-will, all of which qualities are tested by Prospero. The selfish action of Hamlet with Ophelia, where Ophelia ends up with only her St Valentine's Day lament, bedded but not wedded, is not wanted here. Real love requires commitment, sharing and self-sacrifice.

The culmination of this third alchemical cycle leads to true knowledge, which is joy and illumination. It is symbolised by the alchemical (or mystical) marriage, announced in the play by the betrothal of Miranda and Ferdinand. The marriage, when it takes place, will then become the starting point for the fourth cycle, the cycle of the adept, if the initiates so will it and make the necessary effort.

(4) The Adept

Prospero stands as an allegorical example of the adept. The powers attributed to him, though, are not simply allegorical but can be very real in the hands of a genuine adept. No one should be mistaken about this. But the true adept, whilst developing his or her powers, is also learning to work in concert with the ultimate law of life—the law of love. All other laws flow from this supreme law, and the adept has to learn to operate and reconcile the two seemingly contrary laws, the law of justice (or karma) and the law of mercy (or redemption). The latter is the greater law, but in no way should it, or can it, be used at the expense of justice. Mercy transcends justice and transforms karmic situations into different and more blessed conditions, but it does not replace justice. These two great laws seem like opposites, which they are, yet both are necessary parts of the one supreme law of love. The adept has to learn to operate consciously with both laws, balancing them in perfect harmony.[13]

Justice, which disciplines and purifies, is the first to be concentrated upon, and this leads on to the application of mercy, which illuminates and heals. Hence the play begins with Prospero's intention to bring about justice—to right wrongs and, at the same time, to stimulate repentance in the evildoers so that a transmutation of character can take place. This transmutation, with an accompanying new life, can only be completely accomplished when total forgiveness of sins is offered. This merciful act is the fulfilment of love, which gives new life. It is the real 'breath' or 'wind' that fills the island with its sweetness—the breath of life, the breath of love, the breath of God.

Understood rightly, Prospero's justice and apparent severity is not without love, and is simply the necessary prelude to mercy. From the start Prospero's intentions were noble:-

> *Pros.* Be collected,
> No more amazement: tell your piteous heart
> there's no harm done…
> I have done nothing but in care of thee
> (Of thee my dear one; thee my daughter) who
> Art ignorant of what thou art, naught knowing

The Four Levels of Human Evolution

> Of whence I am: nor that I am more better
> Then Prospero, Master of a full poor cell,
> And thy no greater Father.[14]

> The direful spectacle of the wracke which touched
> The very virtue of compassion in thee:
> I have with such provision in mine Art
> So safely ordered, that there is no soul —
> No, not so much perdition as an hair
> Betid to any creature in the vessel…[15]

> Though with their high wrongs I am struck to th'quick,
> Yet, with my nobler reason, 'gainst my fury
> Do I take part: the rarer action is
> In virtue than in vengeance: they being penitent,
> The sole drift of my purpose doth extend
> Not a frown further.[16]

Prospero is an alchemist: his intentions are to transform the base metal of the human psyche into the gold of the pure and illumined soul. For himself personally, he is beyond the stage known in Alchemy as 'The Greater Work', in which the transformation is entirely personal. Instead, he has entered 'The After Work,' in which his noble and illumined soul can project (*i.e.* shine) its virtue to others and help to bring about transformation and transmutation in other people's characters. Some of the stages of transmutation of the human character, from ignoble to noble, can be difficult and even painful, but how we view it is largely a question of consciousness, as pointed out by the experienced philosophers, St Paul, Seneca, Francis Bacon and Peter Deunov:-

> For all things are for your sakes, that the abundant grace might, through the thanksgiving of many, redound to the glory of God.
> For which cause we faint not; but though our outward man perish, yet the inward man is renewed day by day.

For our light affliction, which is but for a moment, worketh for us a far more exceeding and eternal weight of glory...[17]

It was an high speech of Seneca (after the manner of the Stoics), that the good things which belong to prosperity are to be wished, but the good things that belong to adversity are to be admired... Certainly if miracles be the command over nature, they appear most in adversity. It is yet a higher speech of his than the other... It is true greatness to have in one the frailty of a man and the security of a god... The virtue of prosperity is temperance; the virtue of adversity is fortitude, which in morals is the more heroical virtue... Certainly virtue is like precious odours, most fragrant when they are incensed or crushed; for prosperity doth best discover vice, but adversity doth best discover virtue.[18]

Only through trials and tribulations does one come to understand the true nature of love, faith and hope. Only in this way does one understand that love is stronger than lack of love, than hell and death; that faith is stronger than doubt; that hope is stronger than despair; that good is stronger than evil.[19]

These are perceptive thoughts which are echoed in the moralising of the Virginia Company's *True Declaration*, published in 1610 as a report on the state of the colony and about the events of the shipwreck on the Bermudas:-

Omnis inordinatus animus sibi ipsi fit paena: every inordinate soule becomes his own punishment.[20]

Quae videtur paena, est medicina: that which we accompt a punishment against evill is but a medicine against evill.[21]

The alchemist's medicine is called the Philosopher's Stone, which is none other than the spiritual gold of the refined and illumined soul. This 'gold' is a sun, the true soul, whose radiant light can be shone as a medicine to heal and transform the world. The healing rays of this spiritual light have often been symbolised by the spears carried by the 'Spear-Shakers' such as St George, St Michael, Britannia, Pallas Athena and Apollo, who shake their spears of wisdom and virtue at the dragons of ignorance and vice, in order to bring about a death of the old corrupt nature and a rebirth or resurrection (*i.e.* transmutation) into a newer, more enlightened and more virtuous nature.

(5) The Spirit

Unlike the other human characters on the island, Prospero is master of nature's elements, not subject to them. Yet essentially it is not he that does the work. The work is actually performed by his spirit, Ariel. Prospero sees, designs and commands, but it is Ariel who carries out those commands, which he only does if they are basically good. (Ariel refused to obey the evil commands of the witch, Sycorax.)[22] Although Prospero, as a human being, seems to possess the power to work wonders, the principal power is not really his. He is the director, the artist, applying the power, but the power belongs to, and is, the spirit which Ariel represents and which Prospero completely releases at the end of the play. Such a spirit is the quintessence that all souls seek to find and, finding, learn to release.

7. The Alchemical Progress of Humanity

In each of the four types or levels of life cycle depicted in the play, the characters involved experience the four stages of each cycle in alchemical progression. As already explained, fundamentally this alchemical progression begins with an impulse, followed by desire, thought and action.

Such a life cycle can be of short duration, such as, for instance, wanting to read a book, deciding on which one to read, then picking it up and reading it. Or the cycle could be of much longer duration, such as having a desire to pursue a profession, then studying to become qualified in it, then finally practising it, all of which would take many years or even a lifetime. Each longer cycle is made up of exactly the same number and sequence of stages as each shorter cycle, but includes many shorter cycles within itself. Both ordinary life and initiation progress in reasonably large cycles of time, but such progression depends on lots of smaller cycles making up the bigger stages and leaps of evolution. For instance, to walk from one room to another can take many steps, yet it constitutes but one single journey, or stage of a journey. A cycle of initiation, then, could be imagined as four rooms in sequence (*i.e.* four stages), whilst the four main alchemical levels of life (*i.e.* gross, mundane, virtuous and exalted) could be represented by the four levels of a four-storied building.

The four stages of a life cycle are represented by *earth, water, air* and *fire*, and Shakespeare follows the classical

111

method of utilising the symbols of these alchemical elements in each of the main life cycles illustrated in *The Tempest*. Each group goes through its own series of life cycles concurrently with the cycles being experienced by the other groups. Moreover, each group is living life at a different level to the others. In this way Shakespeare has arranged for the four groups to show the four different alchemical levels of the life cycle which co-exist together, whilst also showing how nature, with an adept's help, can raise a person from one level to a higher one.

1. The Servants

The servants—Stephano, Trinculo and Caliban—go through two gross cycles during the time-period of the play. As for all the characters in the play, and as also in the classical Mysteries of initiation, the cycle begins with a storm or tempest. This tempest represents the death experience, in which the persons involved die to the old state and cycle of existence, and are reborn into a new cycle.

1st Cycle

(1) *Earth.* Stephano and Trinculo are shipwrecked by the tempest and hurled onto what is for them a totally new environment—the island. Caliban is already on the island and his experience of the tempest is less dramatic, yet even for him it begins a new cycle of experience that becomes highly dramatic when he meets those whom the sea has hurled onto the rocky shore.

(2) *Water.* Drenched with rain, Caliban, Trinculo and Stephano meet on or near a shore of the island. To begin with, Caliban and Trinculo, forced together by the cloud-

burst, are terrified of each other. The arrival of Stephano, who is too drunk to be frightened, changes the fear of Trinculo into relief and of Caliban into awe. Mention of the moon stirs deep emotions in Caliban. A strange friendship is then cemented with a material liquor rather than with the true spirit of love, and the three get drunk together on a wine that numbs and drowns their senses. They set off together to explore the island, guided by the 'brave monster' Caliban, and with Caliban taking a new and drunken master (rather than Prospero) and proclaiming the high attainment of life without being anywhere near it himself or realising how it is to be attained:–

> *Cal.*   Freedom, high-day! high-day, freedom! freedom, high-day, freedom![1]

(3) *Air.* In another part of the island, the three servants begin to plot how they might be lords and rulers of the island, making it their island state. Trinculo notices and remarks upon their intoxicated condition, and that if the other two residents of the island (Prospero and Miranda) were like them, how the state of the island would totter:-

> *Trin.*   If th' other two be brain'd like us, the state totters.[2]

Their minds, intoxicated by wine and gross desires, hatch up thoughts of ghastly murder and rapine. Then, pleased with themselves at their plan, they set off to perform their infamous deed, this time with Stephano singing a truth without any idea of its meaning:-

> *Ste.*   Thought is free.[3]

Ariel begins to play Stephano's tune on a tabor and pipe; and Trinculo, the jester, in a moment of inspiration, provides an answer to Stephano's inquiry as to what it might be:-

> *Trin.* This is the tune of our catch, played by the picture
> of Nobody.[4]

(4) *Fire*. Although the three drunk and ill-intentioned servants arm themselves and labour hard to try to reach
Prospero's cell, where they intend to carry out the murder
and rape, they are intercepted by Ariel and led astray.

2nd Cycle

(1) *Earth*. Caliban, Stephano and Trinculo, following Ariel's
music and drum, are led 'calf-like' through a painful *earth*
experience of 'tooth'd briers, sharp furzes, pricking goss
[gorse], and thorns, which enter'd their frail shins' (IV, i, 175-
181). The calf, the young of the bull and cow, is a symbol of
Taurus, an *earth* sign.

(2) *Water*. After being torn by the briers and gorse, the three
conspirators are deposited by Ariel in the 'filthy-mantled
pool beyond [Prospero's] cell, that the foul lake o'erstunk
their feet' (IV, i, 181-184). The difference between this filthy
stinking pool and the lake of fresh clear water in which the
neophytes of the Mystery schools used to ritually bathe as
part of the purification rites is very marked, and it aptly symbolises the difference between the gross and the virtuous
states of being. Since the feet are ruled astrologically by
Pisces, a *water* sign indicative of the emotions, it is also noteworthy that their feet stink nearly as much as the filthy man-
tled pool.

(3) *Air*. However, Ariel cannot keep Caliban, Trinculo and
Stephano in the pool forever, as the cycle of life has to continue. They manage to climb out of the pool, smelling 'all
horse-piss' and, remarkably, still retaining their desire for
murder, rape and governance of the island (although the

desire now seems to be a little abated in Stephano and Trinculo). Caliban again speaks some truth without in the least realising the truth of what he is saying:-

> *Cal.* Be patient, for the prize I'll bring thee to
> Shall hoodwink this mischance...[5]

As they approach Prospero's cell, where they see the rich clothes hung out on a line, Stephano and Trinculo are indeed hoodwinked (a Masonic phrase), and to their deluded eyes the prize of fine apparel is prize enough. They are stopped by the line, tempted by the clothes, and deceived by the idea that, simply by wearing the outer form of rulership and nobility, they will become the noble rulers of the island. In this way their thoughts are completely sidetracked away from murder, and no argument of Caliban's can change their minds.

The line with the clothes on it can refer to a clothesline or a line (lime) tree. The play on words is clearly deliberate, for it is followed up with another Masonic statement, 'We steal by line and level,' spoken by Trinculo.[6] The lime tree (sometimes known as a linden tree) is a symbol of grace, beauty and happiness. Its flowers are reputed to be a cure for epilepsy, which is synonymous with an electrical storm or tempest in the human mind. Those who sit under lime trees are said therefore to be healed to some extent or even cured of epilepsy. Lime also exudes a sticky substance to which flies and such like stick—flies being symbolic of Beelzebub and all his demonic creatures, including evil men. The line, in its other meaning, marks a division or boundary—in this case the boundary between the sacred precinct of Prospero's cell and the rest of the island.

In the ethical sense, as used in Freemasonry's symbolism, the line (vertical) is held to be a measure of man, and represents man's allegorical stature in the sense of uprightness of life and justness of intentions.

(4) *Fire*. The pleasure of dwelling in this delusion is sharply interrupted by spirits in the shape of dogs and hounds, set on them by Prospero and Ariel. They are chased away and once again prevented from carrying out the murder. However, in a little while they are allowed to return to the cell, where Prospero has everything under control and where he pardons and releases everyone. The experience has a sobering effect on all three servants. In particular it has a transforming effect upon Caliban, when he suddenly realises who his real master is and how 'fine' he is—an experience which is consummated in the expression of mercy and love shown to Caliban by Prospero, and the acceptance of Caliban back into Prospero's home and family.

2. The Lords

As mentioned previously (see Chapter 6), the lords are divided into two cliques. The three ruling lords (Alonso, Sebastian and Antonio), who are the 'three men of sin', go through one gross cycle followed by one mundane cycle during the time-period of the play. Concurrently the three attendant lords (Gonzalo, Francisco and Adrian) go through two mundane cycles. Although each clique could be treated separately, yet they undergo their experiences together as one group of six characters. In the second cycle all six experience the purgatorial and purifying process that prepares souls for entry into the Lesser Mysteries of initiation—the ruling lords for the first time, and the attendant lords for the second time.

1st Cycle

(1) *Earth*. The lords are precipitated into their first cycle by the tempest and shipwreck, and, like the servants, find themselves cast up on the rocky shore of the island.

(2) *Water*. The initial reaction to their new condition is, to the ruling lords, one of fear, which leads to sorrow and depression in the king, and to anger in Sebastian and Alonso. Gonzalo, on the other hand, keeps his emotions in check, remaining calm and courageous in the face of what appears to them all as true adversity. As with the servants (see above), the moon, ruler of the waters and emotions, is mentioned, howbeit satirically:-

> *Gon.*   You are gentlemen of brave mettle; you would lift
> the moon out of her sphere, if she would continue
> in it five weeks without changing.[7]

(3) *Air*. For Alonso, Gonzalo and the two other attendant lords, the emotional experience of the shipwreck coupled with the magical influence of the island is too much for them, and they fall asleep—just as do many of those who come under the influence of Hades in his Underworld state of being. But Sebastian and Antonio remain awake and alert. Whilst the others lie dreaming, these two plot murder. Like the servants, they are driven by the desire of ruling a country, and erroneously believe that they have been given the opportunity to bring this about.

(4) *Fire*. With Ariel's musical intervention the actual deed of murder is averted. The king and his attendants are woken up with a start, forcing the two conspirators to dissemble their real intentions. The desire and thoughts of the king once more take prominence, which are to search for his lost son. The lords set off together on this quest, to put this thought into action, but find that they wander the island, lost as it were in a maze.

Exhausted and famished, a banquet of fruits and other delicious food appears before them.

2nd Cycle

(1) *Earth*. However, those who are not in a state of moral purity cannot eat at the table of Jove. The love-feast is too sacred to be sullied by those who are in a state of sin, and who have not been purified or prepared. Thus the banquet vanishes in a tempest of thunder and lightning, and in its stead stands a harpy who, in the manner of a last judgement, denounces the three men of sin and reminds them of their evil deeds. The lords are precipitated into a new cycle of experience.

(2) *Water*. Alonso is terror-struck and rushes immediately to the sea, intending to drown himself and 'there lie muddied' with his son, whom he mistakenly believes is drowned (III, iii, 95-102). The other two 'men of sin' wildly chase after him to the sea, followed by the other three lords.

In this image of the salt sea, Shakespeare employs the symbol of another type of purification ritual used in the classical Mysteries. Salt is a powerful cleansing and whitening agent, whilst salt water is very healing of open wounds.

(3) *Air*. However, Prospero and Ariel have no intention that harm should come to anyone, so we next discover that Ariel has somehow rescued the lords from the sea and led them into 'the line-grove which weather-fends [Prospero's] cell', where they 'cannot budge' until Prospero releases them (V, i, 7-11).

Here we have the same image of the line/lime, to which the impure stick, as in the servants' experience of the *air* stage in their second cycle. We hear that the three men of sin (Alonso, Sebastian and Antonio) are distracted, and that the rest are mourning over them, 'brimful of sorrow and dismay' (V, i, 11-17). We also hear from Prospero that the three men of sin have become 'penitent'—that is to say, they have changed their ways, repenting of their sins and seeking forgiveness (V, i, 28).

(4) *Fire*. In the final stage all the lords are released from the lime grove and brought into Prospero's magic circle, the precinct of the cave. Once there Prospero, as the great judge of the island, first admonishes the three ruling lords and then forgives them. He greets and thanks his old friend Gonzalo, and then welcomes them all, revealing to them who he really is. Their senses are restored and the magic bonds lifted from them in this final judgement. Lastly, as a consummation of this stage and cycle, the curtain of the cell is lifted and the lords are able to look into the cave, as was done in the classical Mysteries. There they see the one who was lost—Ferdinand—restored, as it were to life, and immeasurably happy. Not only this, but they also see Miranda for the first time, and betrothed to the prince. Most importantly, they see love. They are then free to be invited into the cave, to rest and to hear a revelation of Prospero's life.

3. The Lovers

Ferdinand and Miranda undergo the initiations of one virtuous cycle during the play, experiencing what the classical Mystery schools would have called the Lesser Mysteries of initiation.

(1) *Earth*. Like the lords and servants from the ship, Ferdinand is thrown into the cycle through the tempest and shipwreck; but, unlike the others, he makes his way to the shore of the island swimming strongly on the crest of the waves. Once ashore he is met by the invisible Ariel and led by the spirit's music towards the centre of the island. The watchdogs barking and the cockerel crowing are well-known symbols of the approach of dawn—particularly the dawn of the Christ light. The music makes Ferdinand remember his father.

Miranda, on the other hand, has witnessed the tempest from the shelter of her island home, but it causes a tempest within her own being and moves her to demand of her father the answer to her question, 'Why?' In this way her entrance into the cycle is initiated, and is followed by her father recounting to her for the first time the story of her life and that of their servant Caliban, and how they came to be on the island. (But, significantly, he doesn't tell her about Ariel.)

(2) *Water*. As Ferdinand approaches the precinct of the cell, Miranda sees him as if he were 'a thing divine' (I, ii, 421). They meet and fall in love. A joke about language is made— significant because sound, when it is the mutual language of love, is a representation of the Word of God, which is Love.

But, before their emotions carry them away too fast, Prospero steps in and imposes a severe test upon them both, which is basically a test of obedience and willingness to serve. This is exactly the same kind of test as has always been imposed on every neophyte entering into the Mysteries. The test is in the nature of a baptism, being a test of the purity and strength of heart love, of peaceful emotion and of basic good-will in the face of any difficulty, as well as of obedience. Such a test is a discipline, and it is the discipline that makes the disciple, who must be able to be subject to his master and teacher willingly, with goodwill.

Ferdinand has to carry logs to stoke the fire in the cell— a job normally done by Caliban; whilst Miranda must peacefully watch, self-disciplined and obedient to her father, with her faith in his love and wisdom tested to the extreme. The fire in the cell is symbol of the love in the heart, and the fact that Ferdinand is employed in stoking it is expressive of his (and Miranda's) own love-fire being stoked by the experience of discipline imposed upon them both.

At the same time the experience initiates Miranda into her own selfhood and independence from her father, to choose of her own freewill a lover and husband with whom she will set up her own home in her own right. The break is painful for both father and daughter, but necessary. Complementary to this, Ferdinand is aroused into his own selfhood and independence from his parents by recognising the woman to whom he wishes to be wed. For them both, the desire to be free and in love, expressing love and making love, is awakened. Their love-desires inflamed, in heart-felt passion they make their vows of undying love, betrothing themselves to each other.

This stage of testing the purity of hearts and motives, and the refining and strengthening of such love, is brought to a conclusion when Prospero frees Ferdinand from his shackles and, before heaven, ratifies his 'rich gift' (*i.e.* the gift of his beloved daughter) by consenting and thereby giving his blessing to their betrothal.

(3) *Air.* The *air* stage of this cycle of initiation is begun when Prospero says to his daughter and future son-in-law:-

> *Pros.* Fairly spoke.
>   Sit, then, and talk with her; she is thine own.[8]

This talking together initiates the development of under-standing between the two lovers. To assist this, Prospero conjures up a masque for the two lovers to watch and learn from. The masque is a Mystery, a 'most majestic vision' (IV, i, 118), conjured up in the mind with airy spirits or thoughts as the actors. But what is acted out is a mystery of life itself, with a direct reference to the allegories used in the Greek Mysteries to portray the three realms of spirit, soul and body, the fall (or rape) of the human soul, the cycle of life and nature, and the role of love in all this (see Chapter 9).

(4) *Fire*. When the masque is ended and the vision 'melted into air, into thin air' (IV, i, 150), Ferdinand and Miranda are encouraged by Prospero to retire into his cell, the cave cut in the rock of the island in which burns the fire. Here their love can be put into practice. This is symbolised by the couple playing chess, in which act they are discovered when Prospero lifts the veil to reveal the two lovers to the lords.

The game of chess is a powerful Freemasonic and Rosicrucian symbol. It has Celtic origins as the *gwyddbwyll* board upon which was played the Game of the Goddess—a contest which must be played by all visitors to the Enchanted Castle, and which all those who would marry the queen and be king of the land must win. The board itself, signifying the kingdom, represents the queen and bride.

Miranda, who is the bride and queen of the Enchanted Island, naturally wants her lover and champion to win the game; hence she is willing to allow Ferdinand to win in any way possible, forgiving him for any false moves even before he might (if ever) contemplate such a thing:-

> *Mir.* Sweet lord, you play me false.
> *Fer.* No, my dearest love,
> I would not for the world.
> *Mir.* Yes, for a score of kingdoms you should wrangle,
> And I would call it fair play.[9]

When the veil over the entrance to the cell is lifted, Miranda and Ferdinand are revealed to the lords. Ferdinand is reunited with his father, the king of Naples, who also gains a daughter into the bargain. Joy bursts out, and thankfulness. Ferdinand exclaims that from Prospero he has 'receiv'd a second life' (V, i, 194-195); and good old Gonzalo cries out a blessing and a deep truth to complete the revelation:-

> *Gon.* I have inwardly wept,
> Or I should have spoke ere this. Look down, you gods,

And on this couple drop a blessed crown!
For it is you that have chalk'd forth the way
Which brought us hither.
Alon. I say, Amen, Gonzalo!
Gon. Was Milan thrust from Milan, that his issue,
Should become Kings of Naples? O, rejoice
Beyond a common joy! and set it down
With gold on lasting pillars: in one voyage
Did Claribel her husband find at Tunis,
And Ferdinand, her brother, found a wife
Where he himself was lost, Prospero his dukedom
In a poor isle, and all of us ourselves
When no man was his own.[10]

Alonso, as king and father, completes the blessing:-

Alon. [*To Fer. and Mir.*] Give me your hands:
Let grief and sorrow still embrace his heart
That doth not wish you joy!
Gon. Be it so! Amen![11]

4. The Adept

Prospero, at the commencement of the play, has reached the position of being an adept, but he now has the opportunity to enter the Greater Mysteries of initiation, the exalted cycle of life, and thereby become a master. To do this he has to perform the After Work of alchemy. To a large extent he appears to be in control of all the various situations that arise, but only by comparison with the others. In reality he himself is tested to the extreme and, like everyone else, is entirely dependent on the grace or love of God and the laws of God that do the work. However, divine Grace has also arranged that a human being may become the Artist who can use the powers of creative love with perception and wisdom to bring about developments which are just, useful and good—not

only in himself but in others also, including all other kingdoms of nature. The After Work is this Art, which brings forth
beauty and truth. Moreover, the application of this Art perfects and exalts the soul of the Artist even whilst the Art is
being practised and doing good to others.

Whereas the moon symbolises the alchemical goal to be
achieved by the lords in the Lesser Work of alchemy, and the
sun represents the goal for Ferdinand and Miranda in the
Greater Work, Mercury is the symbol of the After Work.
Mercury, in fact, is the vital agent that makes all work of
transmutation possible, in every stage; but in the After Work
the alchemist attempts to become like Mercury. Alchemically
speaking, Mercury contains all the other planets, including
the sun and moon, which secret is portrayed in its sign.
Mercury can also be understood to represent the rays of the
sun, as the messenger of Light; so the After Work is to do with
the raised, exalted, radiant Sun, whose mercurial rays reach
out and perform the alchemical work.

The opportunity to enter and perform the After Work
does not necessarily arise often, and the young adept must
ensure that the opportunity, when it appears, is not missed. A
state of readiness is part of the adept's requirements concerning himself; thus, if he misses the opportunity when it arises,
he may have to go through another virtuous cycle of initiation
until the ability to be ready is sufficiently developed.

> *Pro.*   I find my *Zenith* doth depend upon
>   A most auspicious star, whose influence
>   If now I court not, but omit, my fortunes
>   Will ever after droop.[12]

(1) *Earth*. Having perceived, through his 'prescience', that the
opportunity has arisen, Prospero initiates the cycle by sum-
moning up the tempest. For this purpose he directs Ariel in
detail as to the work to be done, which Ariel performs 'to

every article' (I, ii, 195). Prospero, as the commanding adept, watches the tempest without being involved in it in the sense of being subject to it; for, as long as he acts as the Artist, he is the master of Ariel and all the elements.

Then, in answer to his daughter's plea, he reveals to her for the first time who he is, who she is, where they have come from and why he has conjured up the tempest.

(2) *Water*. This revelation is immediately followed by the bringing together of Ferdinand and Miranda, in the hope that they will fall in love with each other. That this might and should happen is an integral part of Prospero's prescience, and a vital part of the work that he has to accomplish. At the same time he sees to it that the various lords and servants are launched into their cycles of experience and are given whatever help he, through the services of Ariel, is able to provide. He has to oversee all things simultaneously, as vigilance is part of the adept's lesson that he has to learn in order to become a master.

Having brought Miranda and Ferdinand together, Prospero then tests them in their love, and in such a way as to encourage their love for each other to be increased and to become wise and disciplined. At the same time he does this so as to break his daughter's bonds to him as his child, so that she may become independent of her parent who was both a father and mother to her for virtually all her life. This is an act of love and sacrifice on his part, for he knows that in doing so he will be losing a daughter who is 'one third' of his life; and at this point he has no way of knowing whether the final outcome will be successful or not, or whether he will be rejected or not.

However, the outcome of this stage is successful, and Prospero is able to sanction and bless their betrothal, explaining why he acted as he did. By this time the lords and servants have already been through one complete cycle of their respective experiences, and are in the process of extricating themselves from the sea and the stagnant pool respectively.

(3) *Air*. Prospero, with the help of Ariel, now presents the masque in honour of the betrothal. This he does using the powers of his mind—the actors in the masque being spirits or thought-forms conjured up in his mind and projected into the minds of the young couple, so that both Ferdinand and Miranda can see them clearly and in a simultaneous way. What is imaged is Prospero's own intuitive understanding of the divine plan of life, or that part of it which he desires the couple to see and learn from, presented in an allegorical and entertaining way, as a Mystery.

But then, before the masque is completed, Prospero suddenly becomes aware of Caliban and his fellow conspirators having climbed out of the pool and still determined to carry out their murderous designs. He perceives them on their way to the cell, crudely armed. During the masque Prospero had 'forgot' their 'foul conspiracy' (IV, i, 139). This is such a human trait. It is quite normal for our attention to focus principally on that which is lightest and most beautiful in our selves and our environment, and thereby to miss seeing that which is still dark and ugly. As an adept, Prospero is learning to develop the ability to see clearly into both the light and dark aspects of nature, and this momentary lapse of vigilance is a sharp lesson to him, which arouses his passion, his anger. He has to learn to temper and use this passion wisely, directing it into wise and effective operations.

What Prospero does is to devise and set up a perfect trap for the would-be murderers—one that will not hurt them but will prevent them from committing the murder and rape, whilst at the same time having the possibility of reforming them. Correctly he assesses that the butler and jester are more naturally thieves than murderers, and that only

Caliban is by nature truly murderous but lacks the courage to do such a deed on his own. With Ariel's help, therefore, he hangs some of his lordly clothes upon the line, ready to catch the villains and turn their thoughts with the trumpery.

The villains are indeed stopped by the line, and Prospero then unleashes spirits in the form of hunting dogs to chase them away. Dogs are symbolic guardians of the Mysteries.

(4) *Fire*. Finally, in the last stage that creates the master soul, having now brought everything under control and made ready for the final hour, Prospero releases the others group by group and gives them their freedom. First he frees the lords, then Ferdinand, then Miranda (by agreeing to her betrothal), then the ship and its crew, then the servants. Then he frees Ariel. Finally he prays for his own freedom, to be given through mercy bestowed by us, the spectators of and participants in this Mystery.

An important part of this liberating process is the necessary surrender by Prospero of all his adept's powers, represented by the breaking and burying of his staff and the drowning of his book. This is, in effect, the total surrender or offering of himself upon the altar of love, as a living oblation to truth. As he makes his own will totally one with God's will he is consumed in the fire of divinely human love. He becomes a phoenix. It is this that sets Ariel completely free, for Ariel is the spirit of love ensouled in Prospero. By asking us for mercy, his own love, now fully released, calls forth in response from us the love in our hearts, thereby drawing us towards a likeness of God. This is the alchemy of the master soul, who allows love to do the work freely.

Revelation is the consummation of this last stage, for love in action enlightens, bringing full knowledge of God, or Goodness made manifest. This revelation is represented not only by Prospero revealing himself to the others, as duke of

Milan, but also by the revealing of Miranda and Ferdinand, lost but found again and in a state of love. These revelations are then to be added to by an account given by Prospero of his experience on the island; but this is to take place inside the cell, behind the veil.

Table 1 -- The Alchemical Cycles of The Tempest

Cycle	Degree	Prospero	Ferdinand & Miranda
FIRE			
E X A L T E D	16 FIRE	8. Reunion. Releases Ariel 7. Forgives all, reveals all	
	15 AIR	6. Remembers Caliban 5. Conjures up masque	
	14 WATER	4. Sanctions betrothal 3. Brings Ferdinand and Miranda together	
	13 EARTH	2. Relates history to Miranda 1. Conjures up tempest	
AIR			
V I R T U O U S	12 FIRE		8. Reunited with all 7. Playing chess in Prospero's cell
	11 AIR		6. Enter Prospero's cell 5. Watch masque
	10 WATER		4. Ferdinand tested. Betrothal. 3. Ferdinand and Miranda meet, fall in love
	9 EARTH		2. Ferdinand on island, led by Ariel 1. Tempest: shipwreck. Ferdinand swims to shore

Cycle	Degree	Lords	Servants (1)	Servants (2)
WATER M U N D A N E	8 FIRE	16. What was lost is restored 15. Admonished and forgiven		
	7 AIR	14. Repentant 13. Imprisoned in lime grove		
	6 WATER	12. Rush to sea to drown 11. Desperate		
	5 EARTH	10. Denunciation by Ariel 9. Banquet snatched away		
EARTH G R O S S	4 FIRE	8. Banquet 7. Wander through maze	8. Intercepted by Ariel 7. Set off to find Prospero	16. Released and pardoned 15. Hunted by dogs
	3 AIR	6. Plot to murder Alonso 5. Drowsiness	6. Plot to murder Prospero 5. Drunkenness	14. Hoodwinked by trumpery 13. Stopped by line
	2 WATER	4. Sorrowful at loss of Ferdinand 3. Fearful	4. Drowning senses in wine 3. S & T meet Caliban	12. Crawl out of pool 11. Led into filthy pool
	1 EARTH	2. Shipwrecked on island 1. Tempest	2. Shipwrecked on island 1. Tempest	10. Led through briars 9. Led away by Ariel

8. The Seven Virtues

Spenser's *Faerie Queene*

The theme and structure of the epic poem, *The Faerie Queene*, attributed to Edmund Spenser, provides not only a major source but also an esoteric pattern for Shakespeare's *Tempest*. Spenser was an initiate of Christian Neoplatonism and his writings are steeped in Neoplatonic thought and mysticism, even to the extent of his composing hymns to the Sovereign Good, as did Orpheus. This, and the fact that Spenser enfolded Pythagorean number and geometric harmony as well as Platonic moral and ethical philosophy in his great works, is of particular interest in this study of Shakespeare's *Tempest*.

The Faerie Queene was published in two parts. Part 1 (containing Books 1, 2 and 3) was first published in 1590. Part II, containing the next three books, was published in 1596. The 1st Folio of Spenser's work, including *The Shepheard's Calander* and *The Faerie Queene*, now with seven books, was published in 1611.

In Spenser's *Letter of the Authors, expounding his whole intention in the course of this worke*, written to Raleigh and annexed to *The Faerie Queene*, he explains that his purpose is, by means of the example and influence of the poem, to 'fashion a gentleman or noble person in vertuous and gentle discipline', following the example of previous great poets such as Homer, Virgil, Ariosto and Tasso. For this the author deliberately chose to create an 'Allegorie or darke conceit', a 'historical fiction', with various levels of meaning. In this epic poem the poet sets out to portray allegorically 'in Arthure, before he was King, the image of a brave Knight, perfected in the twelve private morall vertues, as Aristotle hath defined', and who wears the 'armour' of a Christian man as defined by St Paul. The author then goes on to say that he planned to frame the twelve political virtues of Arthur when king in another future epic poem.

The Faerie Queene revolves around the idea that, after his long education by Timon, Prince Arthur sees a vision of the Faerie Queen, is ravished by her beauty and resolves to find her out. When he discovers her, he proves his worth by taking upon himself twelve adventures in her honour, in which, by being tested, he demonstrates the practice of each of the twelve moral virtues, rather in the pattern of Hercules and his twelve labours but set on the moral level rather than on that of the will. By the 'Faerie Queen' the poet means 'Glory' in his general intentions, and by 'Prince Arthur' he means 'Magnificence'; which latter virtue 'is the perfection of all the rest, and containeth in it them all'. To make the poem more interesting, the poet invents twelve other knights to represent Arthur, as the 'Patrons' of the various virtues.

The 'Letter of the Authors' goes on to state that the author's intention is that the twelfth book, the last, should in fact be the beginning of the history, depicting the twelve-day Annual Feast of the Faerie Queen. At this feast a 'tall clownish young man', rustic like a shepherd, prostrates himself before the Queen and desires a boon, so that 'he might have the achievement of any adventure which during that feast might happen'. Twelve adventures then occur, one on each of the twelve days of the feast. The first adventure is that of the Red Cross Knight, the 'Patron of true Holiness' who, entreated and accompanied by the fair lady, Una ('Truth'), and after various lesser adventures, defeats foul error in the form of a dragon and releases Una's kingdom from oppression.

Only six complete 'adventures' or books, each of twelve cantos, and one incomplete book of three cantos (one unfinished), were published. The rest are said to have been burnt in the fire that destroyed Kilcolman Castle in County Cork, Ireland, Spenser's home. This may be true, yet is it? In Christian Neoplatonism there are only seven virtues, not twelve, and they relate symbolically to the seven sacred planets, all of which move and create their patterns of life within the twelve-fold zodiac of stars. These seven relate to the seven days of the week, the seven spheres of life and consciousness, the seven rays of light, and the seven main notes of the musical scale, that are called forth by the seven great Spirits or *Logoi*. Furthermore, out of Aristotle's *Ethics* Spenser only took two of the virtues enumerated, Temperance and Justice. He uses instead the seven virtues as defined by Christianity, only with some of them described under slightly different names to the ones that are normally used.

The Tempest may provide a clue to solving this riddle of *The Faerie Queene*, just as *The Faerie Queene* provides a clue for *The Tempest*, for Shakespeare appears to have employed the same seven-fold scheme in *The Tempest* that is used in *The Faerie Queene*, in exactly the same order, whilst at the same time enfolding the seven-fold scheme within the twelve-fold structure of the characters in the play. Even looking no deeper than the surface, *The Faerie Queene* has a twelve-fold design in its twelve cantos per book; but there is clearly more to it than that.

A clue is in the seventh book of *The Faerie Queene*. The theme of the seventh book, the legend of Constancy, is about the virtue of Faith, which is related in the Neoplatonic scheme to what the Cabalists call Grace or Mercy (and others call Love), represented by the planet Jupiter. The attainment of this state of Grace, which is only reached by embodying the virtue of mercy or love in one's own being, is the highest state of life and knowledge that an individual person can reach—the culmination of the path of enlightenment, leading to freedom from the world of mutability and separateness, and to absorption in the eternity and unity of divine Love.

This state of being Prospero is all set to achieve at the conclusion of *The Tempest*. In *The Faerie Queene*, the seventh book gives the hint that this is indeed the final book, for the subject of the two cantos is the Titaness Change (who is also known as Mutability or Fortune), who aspires to the highest throne of the gods, challenging even Love, the supreme God, and eventually being judged by the supreme Goddess, Nature. The result of the judgement is the declaration that eventually Change shall change even change, and those subject to change, to something quite different:-

> But time shall come that all shall changed bee,
> And from thenceforth, none no more change shall see.
> So was the *Titanesse* put down and whist,
> And *Love* confirm'd in his imperiall see.
> Then was that whole assembly quite dismist,
> And *Natur's* selfe did vanish; whither, no man whist.[1]

Fortune with her Wheel is put down in the place where she rightly belongs, until the time when even she shall be changed to non-change. Love is re-confirmed in the supreme throne of heaven, and Nature (which is linked with change) vanishes. The poet then neatly concludes the book and the whole poem with the aspirational thought, based upon Nature's decree:-

The Seven Virtues

When I bethinke me on that speech whyleare,
Of *Mutabilitie,* and well it way:
Me seemes, that though she all unworthy were
Of the Heav'ns Rule; yet very sooth to say,
In all things else she beares the greatest sway.
Which makes me loath this state of life so tickle,
And love of things so vaine and cast away;
Whose flowring pride, so fading and so fickle,
Short *Time* shall soon cut down with his consuming sickle.

Then gin I thinke on that which *Nature* said,
Of that same time when no more *Change* shall be,
But stedfast rest of all things firmely stayd
Upon the pillours of Eternity,
That is contrary to *Mutabilitie:*
For, all that moveth, doth in *Change* delight:
But thence-forth all shall rest eternally
With Him that is the God of Sabaoth hight:
O that great Sabaoth God, graunt me that Sabaoths sight.[2]

This is pure Neoplatonism as well as Christianity, alluding to the great goal of the philosopher or mystic—conscious union with the Divine in eternal peace: that state of bliss which transcends our mutable world of finite things. This peace is the Sabbath, the Seventh Day of Rest.

Spenser, who was greatly influenced by Francesco Giorgi's *De harmonia mundi* and Dante's *Divine Comedy*, clearly believed, as Giorgi stated, that through the exercise of virtue man can rise to union with the divine intelligences. We can find the identical belief and theme throughout the Shakespeare works, and in particular in *The Tempest.*

To summarise, therefore, *The Faerie Queene* is based upon a framework of twelve books, reduced to seven. These seven books purposely relate to the seven sacred planets and their corresponding virtues, whilst inferring a twelve-fold zodiacal scheme of King Arthur's Round Table. The practice of these

137

virtues leads to union with the Divine. A similar scheme can be found in Shakespeare's *Tempest*.

The Seven-fold Progression in *The Faerie Queene*

The seven sacred planets symbolise seven archetypal or spiritual intelligences which both affect the path of man's soul and at the same time represent the various levels of consciousness and stages on the path of evolution of the human being. Different philosophers have given different orders of these planets, depending on their point of view and what they have discovered. Spenser gives an unusual order of the planets in his *Faerie Queene* that is echoed exactly by Shakespeare in *The Tempest*. These two works suggest that the seven virtues have to be developed in a certain order—usually by the overcoming of the corresponding vices or tests associated with the gaining of the virtues, and always with the help of the unseen angelic intelligence associated with each virtue. (Interestingly, in *As You Like It*, Shakespeare gives a different order of the seven planetary stages.)[3] To begin with, we will look at *The Faerie Queene*, so as to better understand *The Tempest*.

In *The Faerie Queene* each virtue is associated with the story of one of the books and with the chivalrous hero of that book who attains (and therefore represents) that virtue. The following is a list of the seven books and their corresponding theological virtues, angelic orders and cabalistic principles[4]:-

Book 1. The Legend of the Knight of the Red Crosse, or *Of Holiness*

—concerning the Red Cross Knight and Una, the House of Charity, love, the illumination of darkness, the *Monad* (Una).

Virtue   = Charity (Holiness)
Planet   = Sun
              (the Sun of Christian Religion = Charity)
Angelic Order = Powers
Principle   = Beauty

Book 2. The Legend of Sir Guyon, or *Of Temperance*

—concerning Sir Guyon, the House of Alma, the defence of Solar religion, martial firmness, sternness, righteousness, severity, wrath, purification, and the cleansing power of martial fire.

Virtue   = Temperance

Planet   = Mars

Angelic Order = Powers

Principle   = Judgement, Severity, Righteousness

Book 3. The Legend of Britomartis, or *Of Chastitie*

—concerning Lady Britomart, and the white chastity or purity of the Moon.

Virtue   = Prudence (Chastity)

Planet   = Moon

Angelic Order = Angels

Principle   = Foundation, Generation

Book 4. The Legend of Cambel and Telamond, or *Of Friendship*

—concerning Cambel and Telamond, the Caduceus, and the reconciliation of fighting opposites.

Virtue   = Fortitude (Friendship)

Planet   = Mercury

Angelic Order = Archangels

Principle   = Glory, Good Thought,
                 Communication

Book 5. The Legend of Arthegall, or *Of Justice*

—concerning Arthegall and the wise rule of Astraea, melancholy, knowledge, inspiration, highest intellectual insight.

Virtue   = Justice

Planet   = Saturn

Angelic Order = Thrones

Principle   = Intelligence, Knowledge,
                   Understanding

Book 6. The Legend of Sir Calidore, or *Of Curtesie*

—concerning Sir Calidore, the courtly hero, the vision of Venus and the Graces, star of love, gifts of grace, beauty, charm, courtesy, gentleness.

Virtue   = Hope (Courtesy)

Planet   = Venus

Angelic Order = Principalities

Principle   = Victory, Sweet Emotion,
                   Kindness

Book 7. The Legend of *Constancie*

—concerning the goddess Fortune (*i.e.* Change or Muta-
bility) and her attempt to seize Diana's throne, the gods and goddesses, Pan, Love, Nature, the Seasons, Life, Death, the rule and commandment of Jove the king.

Virtue   = Faith (Constancy)

Planet   = Jupiter

The Seven Virtues

Angelic Order = Dominions
Principle   = Grace, Mercy

Spenser gives a planetary order of the Sun followed by Mars, Moon, Mercury, Saturn, Venus and Jupiter. This clearly has a significant and particular intention and meaning, and it is useful to compare this order with that of: (a) the alchemical process, wherein the stages of alchemy are usually represented in evolutionary order by Saturn, Jupiter, Moon, Venus, Mars, Sun and Mercury; and (b) the hierarchical order of the heavens, signified in ascending order by the Moon, Mercury, Venus, Sun, Mars, Jupiter and Saturn. Spenser does, however, follow the usual division of the seven into (i) two groups, expressing the trinity and the quaternary; and (ii) three groups—the first of three virtues, the second of three virtues, and the third of one virtue. He cleverly does this by creating two parts to *The Faerie Queene*, with three books (1, 2, 3) in Part 1 and four books (4, 5, 6, 7) in Part 2, but setting apart the seventh book in its own right by making it seem to be unfinished and radically different to all the others.

The theme of Spenser's planetary order would seem to indicate that all proceeds from the spiritual Sun, the Light of God, which is the *Monad* or Unity of all life, and culminates in its final and profoundest expression as the jovial quality of Mercy—the Grace, Compassion or Love of God poured out to others constantly. This ending brings life back to its beginning again, as the act of mercy is charity, which is the essential nature of holiness or god-likeness with which the sequence begins. Spenser emphasises this by stating in his Letter that he places the last story first.

The Red Cross knight, representative of the human soul, is associated with the primal Unity, the Sun of Righteousness (*i.e.* the Son of God), who goes forth upon his mission to eventually manifest the holiness of God and his own essential divinity as constant, unfailing compassionate love. To do this the knight (either as male or female) must pass through five intermediate stages of development, signified by the five planets and virtues that lie between the Sun (Holiness, or Beauty) and Jupiter (Constancy, or Mercy). Every one of the seven stages has its challenges to overcome, testing the knight as to his mastery and embodiment of the virtue associated with that stage. Moreover, in each case it is the virtue (or angel) that does the testing.

Thus, after the initial test of charity or holiness, there is a stage of fiery purging and discipline, testing the virtue of temperance. This is followed by a test of chastity or purity (prudence), then a test of friendship (fortitude). After this comes justice, to challenge and test the qualities of the soul so far developed. Then comes a test in courtesy (hope), in which true love could now be developed and made known on a foundation of temperance, chastity and friendship. This culminates with the test in constancy, or mercy—the true Faith in which one realises the eternity of Love and the transience of all else.

The Seven-fold Progression in *The Tempest*

This pattern in *The Faerie Queen* is reiterated in *The Tempest*, but whereas Spenser only gives one cycle of this seven-fold sequence, Shakespeare provides a double cycle. First, a tempest begins the play, inaugurating a new cycle; then follow the planetary stages, showing both the virtues and the vices:-

1st Cycle

Stage 1: Sun–Holiness–Charity–Beauty

Act i, sc. 2. Before Prospero's Cell

Prospero (the Red Cross knight), Miranda (the virgin Una or Truth) and Caliban (the monster or dragon): a time of remembrance and revelation. Here there is a representation of St George and the dragon in the theme of Prospero and Caliban, with Miranda personifying the virgin who is set free by the Red Cross knight from the clutches of the dragon. This is an allegory of the fundamental Rosicrucian theme of Truth being brought forth by Time, and states the purpose of the whole play. Prospero's cell is an emblem of the heart, the sacred space whose fire within it represents the pure love-light that is the divine, incarnate Sun.

Stage 2: Mars–Temperance–Discipline–Judgement

Act i, sc. 2 (cont.)

Ariel leads Ferdinand to Miranda. Fiery love is awakened but immediately tempered by the discipline to which Prospero puts Ferdinand—namely, the carrying of logs to feed the fire (of love) in the cell. Ferdinand, when challenged by Prospero, is aroused to anger and draws his sword (a martial image), but is overcome by Prospero's greater magical power represented by Prospero's staff. The labour of carrying logs disciplines the hot martial energies and sexual drive, transforming them into a patient and potent love.

Act ii, sc. 1. The shore of the island

The lords are angry, the king despondent. Some lords fight with words, taking sides, placing blame, losing their temper. Only Gonzalo remains temperate. Adrian, Antonio and Sebastian bring in a mention of Temperance:-

> *Adr.* It must needs be of subtle, tender and delicate temperance.
>
> *Ant.* Temperance was a delicate wench.
>
> *Seb.* Ay, and a subtle; as he most learnedly delivered.

Stage 3: Moon–Chastity–Prudence–Generation

Act ii, sc. 1 (cont.)

Gonzalo and the king sleep. Antonio and Sebastian stay awake, plotting murder so as to gain the crown, revealing the impurity of their desires and thoughts, which are far from chaste.

Stage 4: Mercury–Friendship–Fortitude–Good Thoughts

Act ii, sc. 1 (cont.)

Gonzalo and the king awake. Antonio and Sebastian, prevented from murder, pretend to be friends of the king and Gonzalo, feigning to have guarded them whilst they were asleep. They are all affrighted by the roars and bellowing as of wild beasts on the island, and run away in a poor show of bravery.

Stage 5:
Saturn (Satan)–Justice–Understanding

Act ii, sc. 2. Another shore of the island

Caliban, in a satanic mood, curses Prospero. Stephano and Trinculo meet Caliban, a very 'devil' who tempts them to ignoble, unjust, unintelligent thoughts. Stephano (another type of devil) tempts them all with base spirit, sack from a bottle, with which they become drunk and befuddled.

Stage 6:
Venus–Courtesy–Hope–Sweet Emotion

Act iii, sc. 1. Before Prospero's Cell.

Ferdinand and Miranda converse whilst Ferdinand bears the logs. They are courteous to each other, making love with their eyes and words. Ferdinand calls Miranda his 'sweet mistress'—an allusion to Venus and the sweet emotion of love. They declare their love for each other, betrothing themselves in marriage and holding a vision of hope for the future.

Stage 7: Jupiter–Constancy–Faith–Mercy

Act iii, sc. 2. Another part of the island

Caliban, Trinculo and Stephano plot to murder Prospero and rape Miranda in most grotesque and heartless ways. Yet, whilst giving way to wholly unloving, unmerciful passions and thoughts, Caliban describes the Jovian blessings of the island as 'sounds and sweet airs, that give delight, and hurt not,' and 'riches ready to drop' upon him.

Act iii, sc. 3. Another part of the island

The lords, having trod a 'maze' and become exhausted and famished, are confronted with a banquet strewn with the gifts of the island. They refer to the harmony or blessing of the banquet scene and remark on the marvellous sweet music. Sebastian and Gonzalo both make a declaration of faith:-

> *Seb.*   Now I will believe
> That there are unicorns; that, in Arabia,
> There is one tree, the phoenix' throne; one phoenix
> At this hour reigning there....
> *Gon.*   Faith, sir, you need not fear.

Gonzalo clearly refers to the teaching of Jesus of Nazareth, who preached that faith, which is merciful and constant love, or goodwill, casts out all fear. The apparition of this Jovan feast vanishes as miraculously as it appeared, amidst the lightning and thunder of Jupiter. A second (psychological) tempest follows.

2nd Cycle

Stage 1: Sun–Holiness–Charity–Beauty

Act iii, sc. 3 (cont.).

Ariel appears in the form of a harpy, a minister of Fate or Destiny, denouncing the 'three men of sin', recounting to them their ugly, unholy deeds, and warning them that the only way to be protected from the wrath of the powers of Fate is a purifying path of heart-sorrow with a 'clear life ensuing'. The dragon of the three men of sin is now in the power of the Rose Cross knight, Prospero. Gonzalo, inspired with dread, remarks:-

Gon.   I' the name of something holy, sir....

Gonzalo again refers to biblical teaching, which proclaims that 'Holy, holy, holy, is the Name of God'. That which is holy is God, the All-Good, signified by the Name of God.

Stage 2:
Mars–Temperance–Discipline–Judgement

Act iii, sc. 3 (cont.).

In an affrighted, desperate ecstasy, the three men of sin rush for the sea, with Sebastian and Antonio, swords drawn, fighting the legions of airy 'fiends':-

Seb.   But one fiend at a time,
          I'll fight their legions o'er.
Ant.   I'll be thy second.
Gon.   All three of them are desperate: their great guilt,
          Like poison given to work a great time after,
          Now 'gins to bite the spirits. I do beseech you,
          That are of suppler joints, follow them swiftly,
          And hinder them from what this ecstasy
          May now provoke them to.

Act iv, sc. 1. Before Prospero's Cell.

Prospero gives the reason for his austere punishment of Ferdinand:-

Pros.   If I have too austerely punished you,
          Your compensation makes amends; for I
          Have given you here a third of mine own life,
          Or that for which I live; who once again
          I tender to thy hand: all thy vexations

Were but trials of thy love, and thou
Hast strangely stood the test...

Stage 3: Moon–Chastity–Prudence–Generation

Act iv, sc. 1 (cont.).

Prospero ratifies the betrothal of Miranda to Ferdinand, and warns against breaking her 'virgin-knot' before all 'sanctimonious ceremonies may with full and holy rite be minister'd'. As he summons up a masque, Prospero again urges the young couple to be chaste:-

> *Pros.*　Look thou be true; do not give dalliance,
>   　　Too much the rein: the strongest oaths are straw
>   　　To th' fire in th' blood: be more abstemious,
>   　　Or else, good night your vow!
> *Fer.*　I warrant you, sir,
>   　　The white cold virgin snow upon my heart
>   　　Abates the ardour of my liver.

Stage 4:
Mercury–Friendship–Fortitude–Good Thoughts

Act iv, sc. 1 (cont.).

Before the masque is finished, Prospero suddenly remembers the approaching danger of Caliban and his two 'foul confederates'. He dismisses the spirits of the masque and prepares himself to meet with Caliban, with whom he must somehow find a friendly resolution, bringing together in harmony the antagonistic opposites or polarities which he and Caliban each represent (symbolised by St George and the dragon, or by St Michael and Satan). For this he needs fortitude and some mercurial cleverness or trickery.

Stage 5:
Saturn (Satan)–Justice–Understanding

Act iv, sc. 1 (cont.).

Caliban, Stephano and Trinculo approach Prospero's cell stealthily, intending murder and rapine. They are stopped by the line of glistering apparel, with which Sebastian and Trinculo are completely seduced, lacking the understanding of Caliban concerning the need for haste and surprise. They are chased away and hunted by dogs and hounds (of Hell). At this hour all the enemies of Prospero (who is in the role of Midas, or Hades, lord and judge of the Underworld) lie at his mercy.

Act v, sc. 1. Before Prospero's Cell.

Ariel reports that the lords are Prospero's prisoners in the lime-grove.

Stage 6:
Venus–Courtesy–Hope–Sweet Emotion

Act v, sc. 1 (cont).

Ariel evokes tender affection in Prospero for those who are now in his power:-

> *Ari.* … Your charm so strongly works 'em,
>   That if you now beheld them, your affections
>   Would become tender.
> *Pros.* Dost thou think so, spirit?
> *Ari.* Mine would, sir, were I human.
> *Pros.* And mine shall.
>   Hast thou, which art but air, a touch, a feeling
>   Of their afflictions, and shall not myself,
>   One of their kind, that relish all as sharply
>   Passion as they, be kindlier mov'd than thou art?

Stage 7: Jupiter–Constancy–Faith–Mercy

Act v, sc. 1 (cont).

Prospero now moves towards the greatest possible act of justice—that of mercy and self-sacrifice, requiring the utmost constancy and faith in the power of love. First he declares his willingness to act with full mercy; secondly he renounces his magic, and thirdly he restores the lords to their senses, releasing and forgiving them entirely:-

> *Pros.* … The rarer action is
>   In virtue than in vengeance: they being penitent,
>   The sole drift of my purpose doth extend
>   Not a frown further. Go release them, Ariel:
>   My charms I'll break, their senses I'll restore,
>   And they shall be themselves.

Finally, Prospero releases Ariel and calls upon us, in our mercy, to release him.

Prospero's work is now complete. Thanks to Prospero's merciful justice, bestowed with love, wisdom and power, all the characters step into Prospero's cell, beyond the veil, thereby entering (in various degrees or conditions) the glorious solar state of Unity and Holiness. An explanation or revelation will be given, a sea-journey is to be undertaken, and a future cycle will be inaugurated, as Fortune turns her wheel and Time continues to bring forth more and more beauty and truth.

9. The Three Kingdoms

Shakespeare has set the scene of *The Tempest* not only on an island but also within a landscape that embraces three cities and kingdoms. These are Milan, Naples and Tunis. Prospero is duke of Milan, Alonso is king of Naples, and Alonso's daughter Claribel has just become queen of Tunis. The historical associations and geographical locations of these are highly significant, and Shakespeare has clearly noticed this and selected them for his play as a result. These cities form a triangle with each other (with points north-east-south), with Milan located in northwestern Italy, Naples on the west coast of southern Italy, and Tunis on the north coast of Tunisia (Africa). They were founded by the Romans, Greeks and Phoenicians respectively. In their relationship to each other they form the foci of what could be called a landscape temple, in which the Mystery takes place.

Milan

Milan used to be called *Mediolanum* by the Romans, and at one time it was known as the New Athens, being a famous centre of culture and learning. It was founded with a boar sacrifice and dedicated to Minerva (*i.e.* Pallas Athena, the Spear-Shaker). Located in a beautiful plain, it was originally a city of Cisalpine Gaul that was founded by Gallic invaders,

THE THREE KINGDOMS

the Biturges, led by Bellovesus. The Romans captured the city in 222 BC, and in the course of time it became the residence of the emperors of the Western Empire, until the invasion of Attila in AD 450-452 caused the Romans to move their imperial headquarters to Ravenna. During the time that the city was the imperial residence it became such a famous centre of culture and learning that it was referred to as the New

Athens. The city revived under the Ostrogoths, but later fell
to the Burgundians and lost its splendours.

Milan thus had three major cultural periods or lives, reviv-
ing its splendours twice but dying to them the third time. It is
therefore interesting in this context that Prospero says that he
will 'retire me to my Milan, where every third thought shall be
my grave' (V, i: 310-311). Prospero seems to be alluding to the
third degree of initiation in which, in Craft Freemasonry and
the Ancient Mysteries, the initiate learns to die.

Naples

Naples, or Neapolis, was founded in the 6th century BC by
the Chalcideans of Cumae on an ancient site called
Parthenope (after the siren of that name), located at the head
of a beautiful south-facing bay and on the western slope of
Mount Vesuvius. The Chalcideans were Greek (Ionian)
colonists and the city, therefore, was one of Greek culture,
renowned for its beauty, its music, its schools and its gentle
climate. It continued to be a Greek city even after it passed
into the hands of the Romans in 328 BC. Its beautiful scenery
and the luxurious life of its inhabitants made it popular with
the Romans, and this popularity continued into later times.

Cumae, the mother town of Neapolis, founded c. 1050
BC, was the most ancient of all the Greek colonies in Italy and
Sicily. Located a short distance to the northwest from
Neapolis, it was built on a steep hill of Mount Gaurus, a little
north of the Misenum promontory. It was the residence of
the earliest oracular Sibyl (Prophetess), who dwelt in the
Cumaean cave, and was the gateway to the great Mystery
school that flourished there in underground caverns and
hidden valleys of the mountain. Æneas consulted the
Cumaean Sibyl before he descended into the underworld of
the Mystery school.

Naples became an independent dukedom in the 8th century AD. In 1139 it was annexed to the kingdom of Roger de Hauteville, the 'great count' of Sicily who had assumed the style of a king in 1130 and who welded the south of Italy and Sicily into one political unit, the kingdom of the Two Sicilies. To distinguish that part of the Sicilian kingdom that lay on the mainland of Italy from that of the island of Sicily, the mainland part was called the kingdom of Naples. In 1266 Charles of Anjou, brother of Louis XI of France, overthrew the Hohenstaufens and made Naples the capital of his kingdom. Under Charles and his Angevin and Aragonese successors, the city grew and flourished in trade and commerce, although for a short time the Sicilian kingdom was divided into two by war and political intrigue. Alphonso 'the Magnanimous' became king of Naples in 1443, and under his rule Sicily was once again united to Naples and a new, enlightened era was inaugurated. With his death in 1458, however, the kingdom of the Two Sicilies was divided between his successors. In 1522 the kingdom of Naples became a possession of the Spanish Hapsburgs.

Tunis

Tunis, the capital of Tunisia, is situated on an isthmus separating two salt lakes and at the mouth of the river Catada, which flows into the Mediterranean Sea. It was not the original capital of the African kingdom, however, but took over from Carthage when Arabs destroyed the latter city in AD 698.

Carthage, the original capital and a port, was located ten miles northeast of Tunis, on the shore of a great bay. One of the most celebrated cities of the ancient world, it was founded *c.* 853 BC under the name of Byrsa by Phoenician colonists fleeing from Tyre. They were led by Elissa, daughter of Belus, king of Tyre, who became their first queen—Queen Dido.

According to Virgil, Æneas met and married Dido when he came to Carthage, and she committed suicide when he departed for Cumae. (See Chapter 3.) The Carthaginians became pre-eminent in commerce and agriculture amongst the nations of the ancient world, their land and shores being rich in corn, herds, fish and oil, and their port being a major trading post on the Phoenician trade route, situated midway between the eastern and western halves of the Mediterranean. It passed into Roman hands in AD 146, after the third Punic war between the Carthaginians and Romans, and became the second city of the Latin part of the Roman Empire.

With the conquest by the Arabs in the 7th century, the Carthaginian province was effectively taken over and run by the Berbers, and Islamic religion was established rapidly. Eventually, in 1336, Abu Zakariya, prince of Tunis, proclaimed independence from the Arab overlords, and founded a dynasty (the Hafsids) that lasted until the 16th century, when the Turks took over. Under Turkish rule, Tunisia became in effect a pirate state.

The Temple of the Human Body

These three capitals and their kingdoms have a direct relationship to the three principal parts of the human body and the worlds to which they relate. For instance, the essential form of the human body is composed of a head, chest and abdomen. Without these we cannot physically survive. Our arms and legs are useful but not essential to us in the same way as are our head and torso. Expressing life's law of polarity, the head and abdomen form polarities to each other—the skull being a fairly rigid structure, protecting the brain within it, and the abdomen being a fairly flexible and fleshy part of the body, able to expand and contract with ease. The chest is the balance of the two, lying in between head and abdomen, and with its rib cage being partly flexible and part-ly rigid and protective. Moreover, each of these (head, chest or abdomen) contains a major group of organs. The head contains the organs of perception, cognition and communi-cation, and is the focus of thought. The chest contains the organs of life (*i.e.* lungs and heart), and is the focus of love and emotion. The abdomen contains the organs of procre-

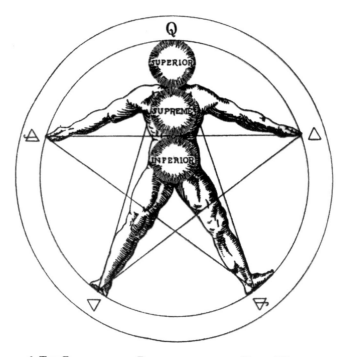

6. THE PYTHAGOREAN PENTALPHA AND THE THREE WORLDS

Illustration from John Reuchlin's *Explication of the Pythagorean Doctrine* as illustrated in Manly P. Hall's *Man: Grand Symbol of the Mysteries*, Chapter III, 'The Mystery of the Three Worlds'.

ation, assimilation and excretion, and is the focus of will power and action.

Neoplatonic tradition refers to these three areas of the human body as the supreme (chest), superior (head) and inferior (abdomen) realms, and relates them to the three worlds of spirit, soul and body, known as the spiritual world, the celestial world and the natural world respectively. The creative rhythm of life moves through the body in this same order, from heart to head to abdomen, as the process of desire, thought and action. In initiation this becomes loving, understanding and service. In terms of our human evolution, however, the order is reversed: for first we begin as a brute-man, then evolve into an intellectual person, and finally become an intuitive or spiritual person, climbing in our consciousness through the three worlds, from natural to celestial to spiritual. In the body these areas do not form a linear progression, such as rising from abdomen through the chest to the head. Instead they form what is known as a mercurial movement. In this lies a great secret of life that is not immediately obvious to just a cursory glance and assumption.

It is therefore noteworthy that Milan, the most northerly metropolis of the three capital cities, was renowned as a city of culture and learning, dedicated to Minerva (Pallas Athena), the goddess of learning, patroness of the Arts and Sciences, and Tenth Muse. Moreover, it was founded by the light-skinned Gauls and subsequently developed by the Romans, who were renowned for their law, order, discipline and martial traits. All these are attributes of the mind and head.

By contrast, Tunis is the most southerly metropolis of the three, its fame being due in the past to its agricultural and mineral wealth, its economic prosperity and its commercial trade. The goddess of its original, Carthage, was a very human one, Dido, who became known as the 'Widow' and

'Mother' of the initiates. Carthage was founded by the Phoenicians, and Tunis by the dark-skinned African Berbers and Arabs, who were renowned for their ability as traders and in the sensuous arts. Wealth, trade and sensuality are associated with the abdomen area of the body.

Naples, midway between the other two, has the distinction of being associated with the Mystery centre of Cumae and its Sibyl or Oracle, as well as being a place of great harmony and beauty, beloved of Greeks and Romans alike. It was a thriving centre of both culture and trade, but most of all of music, love and enjoyment. It was founded by the Greeks, a golden-skinned people, who artistically blended the severity and discipline of learning with the more relaxed mode of sensual living. Such harmony, balance, beauty and music are attributes of the heart and chest area of the body.

The skin-colouring of the races who founded the cities additionally form part of the symbolism, for the alchemical symbols for the three worlds and levels of human development associated with these areas of the body are the colours black, white and red, or the equivalent symbolic metals lead, silver and gold.

The Masque

Shakespeare adds to this in the masque conjured up by Prospero (IV, i, 60-142) for the benefit of Ferdinand and Miranda. The masque features the three goddesses, Iris, Juno and Ceres. Iris, the rainbow goddess or 'heavenly bow' is the 'many coloured messenger' of the gods, and in particular of Juno in this masque. She is the feminine counterpart of Mercury (Hermes). Juno (Hera) is the wife or feminine counterpart of Jove (Jupiter/Zeus). Jove and Juno rule the spiritual world, referred to as 'heaven' in common parlance. Ceres (Demeter) and her masculine counterpart Neptune

(Poseidon) rule the celestial world of the soul, commonly referred to as 'world'. 'Dusky Dis' (Pluto/Hades) and Vesta (Hestia) rule the 'underworld' or natural world.[1]

Ceres refers to her daughter whom 'dusky Dis' abducted. Her daughter is Proserpina (Persephone), who became queen of the underworld. Ceres also refers to Venus and her son, the 'blind boy', who 'did plot the means that dusky Dis [her] daughter got'. Venus' son is Cupid (Eros). There are two Cupid's in classical tradition. The first is the original God, the 'First-Born' and god of all other gods. This is divine Love, also known as the Logos or Word of Wisdom. This Love is the Creator, who 'out of Chaos begot all things, the gods included'.[2] The attributes assigned to him 'are in number four: he is always an infant; he is blind; he is naked; he is an archer'.[3] The second Cupid is the youngest of all the gods, and is the son of Venus. To him 'the attributes of the elder are transferred, and whom in a way they suit'.[4] Just as the first Cupid signifies the First Cause or Alpha of Creation, so the second Cupid signifies the Omega or final result of creation. This Omega is the enlightened human soul, the 'image' of God.

The second Cupid, the human soul, is associated with scandal, because in the course of human evolution the soul's love and wisdom is imperfect, and the aim of his/her heart, which shoots the arrows of desire and love, is often wide of the mark. Yet ultimately this young Cupid will come of age and be a true individual representative of the elder universal Cupid. The young Cupid is the adept, the human soul that is reborn or resurrected from the lower self or psyche. He is also known as Dionysus, or Bacchus, in the Greek Mysteries, and as Mercurius (Mercury) in the Roman version of the Mysteries.

The imagery of the reapers in the masque point to the means by which the second Cupid is born, which is (symbolically) on the winnowing fan after the harvest is reaped and the corn threshed. This symbolism is used in both the Greek (Orphic) and Christian Mysteries. The emblem known as the 'Cupid', 'Blind Boy' or 'Archer' headpiece, printed on the first page of *The Tempest* in the Shakespeare folio, represents this Cupid being born from the cornucopia of nature, but with grapes being used in the cornucopia rather than a sheaf of corn.[5] The sheaf of corn, however, is shown in the AA headpiece in the Shakespeare folio (see Chapter 12, 'The Rosicrucians: The Double A').

Prospero's Island

All these elements, characters, gods and goddesses, are brought together on Prospero's island. For instance, Antonio, as acting duke of Milan, is a human representative of Neptune who, by usurping Prospero's position, sent his brother on his initiatory journey. Alonso, king of Naples, is the counterpart to Jove, and the king of Tunis is the counterpart to Dis. Jove's daughter by Ceres was Proserpine, who married Dis, and she is clearly represented by Claribel who marries the king of Tunis. Prospero would appear to represent Atlas, the 'son' of Neptune and king of Atlantis. According to Eusebius, Atlas was Enoch, the first great Initiate of the human race, whose work now is to help prepare, teach and initiate the rest of mankind—the very role that Prospero acts out in the play.

By his wife, Pleione, Atlas had seven daughters who are represented by the Pleiades, but an older tradition makes them one daughter called Maia, the 'Mother' (Mary), because she became the mother of Mercury, the second Cupid. Maia's husband or lover was Jupiter. In *The Tempest* Miranda appears to represent Maia, whilst Ferdinand, the prince of Naples, personifies that aspect of Jupiter who married Maia. Their child will be, therefore, the second Cupid, whom Prospero is alluding to and celebrating in the masque.

Maia, and therefore Miranda, is the equivalent of Venus. Her symbol is the rose. She represents human love, devotion and beauty—or, as Prospero says, his 'dear heart' (I, ii, 307).

From this point of view Prospero's island really is Atlantis, and Prospero the king of it. The island can also be understood as connected with Paphos, the place that received Venus when she emerged from the foam of the sea, as did Miranda when she first landed on the island, carried in the arms of her father. Paphos was the favourite resort and home of Venus (Aphrodite), and was the chief seat of her worship. In historical rather than mythological terms, Paphos was a Phoenician colony built on the west coast of Cyprus, the fragrant isle. The great temple of Venus, famous in ancient times, stood there, and its high priest was renowned for exercising a kind of religious superintendence over the whole island, just as Prospero does on his island. In the masque Iris says that she met Venus 'cutting the clouds towards Paphos, and her son dove-drawn with her' (IV, i, 93-94). She continues by saying that 'Here thought they to have done some wanton harm upon this man and maid [Ferdinand and Miranda]'. 'Here' could mean Paphos. This is supported by the fact that Cyprus was known as Macaria, 'the happy isle', and Ben Jonson refers to Macaria in his masque, *The Fortunate Isles and Their Union*, in which he both links and satirises Shakespeare's *Tempest,* Bacon's *New Atlantis* and the 'Brethren of the Rosie Cross', and parodies Ariel as Jophiel. In the masque's address to King James, Jonson says:-

When all the fortunate isles should be joined,[6]
Macaria, one, and thought a principal,
That hitherto hath floated as uncertain
Where she should fix her blessings, I tonight

Instructed to adhere to your Britannia.
That where the happy spirits live, hereafter
Might be no question made by the most curious,
Since the Macarii come to do you homage.[7]

10. The Characters

Meanings & Mythology of Names

In all his plays, Shakespeare names his characters with great care, so that the names usually tell something about the character and the part that that character has in the play.

In *The Tempest* there are twelve main human characters plus one leading spirit, Ariel. The master, boatswain and crew of the ship feature at the beginning and end of the story only, and are not main characters. The twelve principal human characters fall naturally into four groups of three that can be seen to represent four levels of human evolution, with all twelve encompassing the development of humanity from brute-man to magus. Whereas Ariel is associated with the quintessence, the Æther, the four human groups can be represented by the alchemical elements. They may also have a zodiacal significance:-

FIRE	Initiates	Prospero	Miranda	Ferdinand
AIR	Lords	Gonzalo	Francisco	Adrian
WATER	Men of Sin	Alonso	Sebastian	Antonio
EARTH	Servants	Stephano	Trinculo	Caliban

Prospero

The name *Prospero* has two derivations from Latin:-

- *Pro-spero. Pro* means 'forward' and *spero* means 'to look for', 'expect', 'hope'. Combined, the name means 'forward looking', 'hopeful', and also 'one who gives hope'.

- *Prosperare,* meaning 'to cause to succeed'. The English word *prosper* is derived from this Latin word, and in this form Prospero is more than once addressed or alluded to in the play. According to the Oxford Dictionary, *Prosper* means '1. To be prosperous, fortunate, or successful; to thrive, succeed, do well. 2. To cause to flourish; to be propitious to.'

Hope is the second of the three qualities or virtues to be developed in the Christian way of life. Faith-hope-charity are the names for the three stages of initiation: namely, (1) learning to love truth (faith), (2) learning to understand truth (hope), and (3) learning to serve truth (charity). Hope is the vision and understanding of truth. It relates to the mind and the faculties of thought-these faculties being imagination, reason and memory. When illuminated by love from the heart, the mind sees love, comprehends love and remembers love: and this is hope. Moreover, according to St Paul in his letter to the Romans, hope saves us,[1] and this is precisely what Prospero achieves through his magic and mercy.

Prosperity is associated with Jupiter and the grace of God. As the all-powerful, wise and generous king, Jupiter bestows wisdom and grace, promoting prosperity. Since Prospero is king of his Atlantean island, the realm of Jupiter, the name is well suited to him. As already pointed out (see Chapter 3, 'The Mysteries: Ogygia'), he acts like Jupiter.

Miranda

The name *Miranda* is derived from Latin *miror*, 'to wonder, be astonished at, admire, look on with admiration'. Our English words *admire and admiration* are derived from this root, as declared by Ferdinand:-

> *Fer.* Admir'd Miranda!
> Indeed the top of admiration! worth What's dearest to the world!...
> ...but you, O you,
> So perfect and so peerless, are created
> Of every creature's best.[2]

Thus the name Miranda means 'admirable, wonderful, pleasing, excellent', the very best of everything. Prospero calls her his 'dear heart' and 'a cherubin':-

> *Pros.* O a cherubin
> Thou wast that did preserve me.[3]

> *Pros.* Awake, dear heart, awake!
> Thou hast slept well;
> Awake![4]

A cherub is one of the great angels of light or wisdom that bring illumination, a messenger of the wisdom and grace of God. They are described in tradition as the lights that flash from the heart of God, establishing the cosmos or throne of God. In terms of the human being, when the heart is fired with love it shines with light and brings illumination to the mind. This light is the cherubic light.

Miranda can be understood, therefore, as personifying Prospero's heart with its love-light that illumines his thinking and blesses his life. It is noteworthy, then, that Miranda was only three years old when Prospero was driven from his dukedom and cast ashore on the island. Prospero says that it was she who saved him. His 'heart' was then only a child, but at least it was awake (alive) with love-light, shining as a cherub that did preserve Prospero.

Then, for twelve full years, Prospero carefully and lovingly nurtured his heart; until at the time the tempest was raised Miranda was fifteen years old. Fifteen is the number of the Rosary, associated with the Virgin Mary, who signifies the pure heart in which the Christ, the love-light and joy of God, is conceived, gestated and born. The pure or virgin heart is the innermost and purest part of the soul. The Rosary represents the wholeness or full development of the heart in love, understanding and service, which sets it on fire with love. In and born from this fire (or flame) is light.

Miranda's mother is hardly mentioned in the play, except once by Prospero ('Thy mother was a piece of virtue...' – I, ii: 56). Clearly we are intended to think that she had died before the usurpation of Prospero's dukedom by his brother, or even that she had died in childbirth when Miranda was born.

Miranda is the only visible woman in the play. All the other characters are men (with the exception of Ariel who is a hermaphrodite spirit, and the other spirits who play goddesses in the masque). This places Miranda in a unique position, like a focal point; which indeed is what Prospero intimates:-

> *Pros.*   I have done nothing but in care of thee,
>   Of thee, my dear one; thee, my daughter, who
>   Art ignorant of what thou art; nought knowing
>   Of whence 1 am, nor that 1 am more better
>   Than Prospero, master of a full poor cell,
>   And thy no greater father.[5]

The attempted violation of Miranda by Caliban is, therefore, a cursed and dangerous matter. The rape of any woman is bad enough, but in the symbolism of *The Tempest* it is doubly bad: for Miranda is that which is most admired and most worthy of admiration. She is the rose of the heart, the jewel of beauty, the Holy Grail or vessel of light, sanctified and blessed by God.

Ferdinand

The name *Ferdinand* is derived from a compound of Old German *fardi*, 'journey', and *nanthi*, 'risk', 'venture'. The name thus means 'venturous life', 'world-daring', 'life-adventuring', 'courageous', 'brave', 'bold'.

Francisco gives a good description of Ferdinand's character when describing how he was the first, in the storm and shipwreck, to fling himself bravely into the surging sea and make for the land:-

> *Fran.*   I saw him beat the surges under him,
> And ride upon their backs; he trod the water,
> Whose enmity he flung aside, and breasted
> The surge most swoln that met him; his bold head
> 'Bove the contentious waves he kept, and oared
> Himself with his good arms in lusty stroke
> To th' shore, that o'er his wave-worn basis bowed,
> As stooping to relieve him: 1 not doubt
> He came alive to land.[6]

Such daring courage and willingness, even delight, in taking on new journeys and challenges in life is a necessity for the soul who is undertaking initiation. In fact, initiation cannot take place without this quality, which is essentially a quality of the heart, symbolised by the lion. There is no room for fear, for fear is a lack of faith or love. The very first degree of initiation is a test in faith, which is the courage or strength

The Wisdom of Shakespeare in *The Tempest*

of the heart to face up to and surmount all challenges which life might present. Such a person knows deep within that all is well, seeking life and love but not minding whether he/she lives or dies: for there is no fear of death, only trust in God and God's love.

Ferdinand is, therefore, the right match for Miranda, the two together signifying the compassion and courage of the true heart, which manifests the wisdom and intelligence of the divine heart.

Gonzalo

The name *Gonzalo* is derived from Latin *com*, 'with', and *salo*, 'salt'. The name therefore means 'with salt'.

Salt is a symbol for a pure-hearted and wise person, particularly in the sense of worldly-wise or wise on all levels of being. Salt also signifies hospitality, durability and purity. To eat bread and salt together was once considered to make an unbreakable league of friendship. Salt is used for preservation, for purification, and for bringing out the flavour in certain foods. Hence Jesus said to the people on the Mount of Beatitudes:-

> Ye are the salt of the earth: but if the salt have lost its savour, wherewith shall it be salted? It is thenceforth cast out, and to be trodden under foot of men.[7]

Gonzalo is clearly one of those men who might well be called the salt of the earth. He appears to be a good councillor and faithful servant to the king of Naples, and a friend to all. Although he had to carry out the orders of his king when Antonio usurped his brother's position, yet he was as much a friend as he could be to Prospero, making sure that Prospero and his little daughter were as comfortable as circumstances allowed, and that Prospero had his precious

168

books with him. Indeed, without Gonzalo's charity, Prospero and Miranda might never have survived their ordeal.

> *Pros.* Some food we had, and some fresh water, that
> A noble Neapolitan, Gonzalo,
> Out of his charity, who being then appointed
> Master of this design, did give us, with
> Rich garments, linens, stuffs and necessaries,
> Which since have steaded much; so, of his gentleness,
> Knowing I lov'd my books, he furnish'd me
> From mine own library with volumes that
> I prize above my dukedom.[8]

Gonzalo is not only thoughtful towards others, trying to help as best he might, but he also claims some knowledge of history and legend. He speaks eloquently and with apparent authority about Widow Dido, Æneas, Carthage and Tunis. However, he is not entirely correct. He confuses Tunis with Carthage, not realising that Tunis was built ten miles south-west of Carthage and only became important after Carthage was destroyed by the Arabs in AD 698. Moreover, his description of a perfect state is clearly ridiculous.

The inaccurate observations, the naive philosophy concerning a utopia, and the remarks about Carthage, identify Gonzalo as a character based on that of the French courtier, philosopher and essayist, Michel de Montaigne. Montaigne was known for his humanity, his descriptions of people, places, current events and history, much of it second or third-hand, and his own inaccuracies of observation. Gonzalo's description of his kind of utopia is a paraphrase of a passage in Montaigne's essay on Cannibals. In the same essay Montaigne comments on Plato's story concerning Atlantis and on a tale concerning the Carthaginians that was supposedly related by Aristotle.

Francisco

The name *Francisco* is Spanish for *Francis*. The Latin, *Franciscus*, was employed to mean 'the Frenchman', but the appellation is derived from Latin *francus*, 'free', which is what the name means. Its secondary meanings are 'liberal', 'bounteous', 'generous', 'friendly'. The word *free* is itself derived from the Sanskrit *pri*, 'to love'. Francis, Frank, French, friend, freedom, etc., are all derived from the same root, and all basically mean 'loving'.

Although Francisco plays a very minor part in the play, his name is that of the great goal of the play—freedom. Therefore it is worth noting what he says. His first speech is the one where he tells the king that he observed Ferdinand swim safely to the shore, alive and well (II, i, 110-118 – see 'Ferdinand' above). No one else had either noticed that fact or thought it possible; and the king and the others ignore what he says.

Francisco's second very short speech is to note something strange about the manner in which the spirits vanish in the banquet scene. This is again something which the others do not notice, and again they ignore Francisco:-

> *Fran.* They vanish'd strangely.
> *Seb.* No matter...[9]

Francisco notices things clearly and in detail. He also speaks the truth.

Adrian

The name *Adrian* is supposedly derived from the Latin *Hadrianus*, meaning 'from the Adriatic'. But the Adriatic is the 'Black Sea', its name being derived from Latin *ater*, 'black', 'dark', 'dead black' (in contr. to *niger*, 'shining black'). Hence the name *Adrian* means 'the Dark One'. The Greek god, *Hades*, the Dark Lord of the Underworld, is associated with this name.

Like Francisco, Adrian has few spoken lines in the play, but what he does speak of concerns place and action. He is also correct concerning Widow Dido and Carthage, whereas Gonzalo is wrong.

> *Adr.* Though this island seem to be desert,
> Uninhabitable, and almost inaccessible,
> Yet it must needs be of subtle, tender and delicate temperance.
> The air breathes upon us here most sweetly.[10]

> *Adr.* Tunis was never grac'd before with such a paragon to their Queen.[11]

> *Adr.* 'Widow Dido' said you? You make me study of that: she was of Carthage, not of Tunis.[12]

> *Adr.* Follow, I pray you.[13]

Alonso

The name *Alonso* is the Spanish version of *Alphonso*, from Old German *Adalfuns*, a compound of *athal*, 'noble', and *funsa*, 'ready', 'apt'. *Alonso* thus means 'noble and ready'.

In the play it is clear that Alonso has not lived up to all that his name means. Far from being noble in character, he has been distinctly ignoble. But, from the point of view of a selfish nobility that acquires what it wants by means of force, armed or otherwise, Alonso does live up to his name. He is very ready to seize every opportunity he can to enlarge and secure his kingdom: firstly with his assistance given to Antonio in deposing Prospero in return for suzerainty over

Milan, and secondly by marrying his daughter Claribel to the king of Tunis against her wishes, for clear political and economic gain. There was, and still is, a certain level of consciousness, widespread in the world, which would consider such actions commendable and even fitting for the ruler of a political or commercial empire, for they would see this as the way to prosper. This is an entirely different kind of prosperity to that represented by Prospero.

It is perhaps Alonso who undergoes the greatest psychological change of all in the play—a veritable 'sea-change' (I, ii, 403).

Sebastian

The name *Sebastian* is derived from Latin *Sebastianus*, referring to 'a man of Sebastia'. *Sebastia* is derived from Greek *sebatos*, meaning 'venerable', respected', and this is the meaning of the name *Sebastian.*

However, even if outwardly Sebastian is a respected man, privately he is more than ready, at Antonio's suggestion, to murder his brother Alonso and seize the kingship.

Antonio

The name *Antonio* is the Italian form of Antony, derived from Latin *Antonius*, meaning 'inestimable', 'priceless'.

The name is associated with two famous saints. One of them, St Antony the Great, was the highly regarded Egyptian hermit, the patron of swineherds, whose symbols are the *Tau* (signifying Truth), a bell and a pig. Significantly, other than Apollo, the most famous swineherd was Merlin, the great magus and teacher of King Arthur, the Boar of Cornwall and archetypal Red (or Rose) Cross Knight. All druids were known as boars and their disciples as pigs—

swine representing the human personality, which was offered as a sacrifice in both the Druidic and the Dionysian Mysteries. Interestingly, pig's lard was used as a remedy for erysipelas, a local febrile disease accompanied by diffused inflammation of the skin which makes the skin look rosy or inflamed, and which was, for these reasons, known as 'St Antony's fire' or 'the rose'.

The other saint, St Antony of Padua, was a friend and disciple of St Francis of Assisi. He was a great scholar and orator, and travelled a great deal on behalf of the Franciscan Order. His special symbols are a flaming heart, a flowered cross and a lily. He is invoked to find lost property.

Camden (1605) derived *Antony* from the Greek word *anqos*, meaning 'the flower', which was specifically used by the Greeks as their name for rosemary. Although this derivation is not incorrect etymologically, it is quite a curious link. *Anthos* was used in England from 1585 as the botanical name for rosemary, the flower *par excellence*. The rose and lily are the primary symbols of the Virgin Mary. Rosemary is Mary's rose, and the rose-lily is a Rosicrucian symbol of the purity and beauty of the heart.

Antonio's name, therefore, appears to be a deliberate Shakespearean satire: for Antonio is clearly not a scholar, is certainly not a Rosicrucian or Merlin figure, and he stole Prospero's property. He tried to kill his brother and brother's child (and believed he had succeeded), and exhorts Sebastian to murder his. He is a thief and a murderer.

This satirical antithesis appears to be a witticism based on the association of *Antony* with *antonym*, meaning 'a term which is the opposite of another', and *antonomasia*, meaning 'the substitution of an epithet, etc., or the name of an office or dignity, for a person's proper name'.[14]

173

Stephano

Stephano, the name of the drunken butler who would be king of the island, aptly means 'crowned one'. The name is derived from Greek *stejanos*, 'crown'.

Stephano as a character demonstrates the complete and, if it were not potentially lethal, ludicrous antithesis to real kingship. Whereas Alonso personifies a typically human kingship, which, although selfish, greedy and dangerous, is nevertheless kingship in a worldly sense, and Prospero demonstrates the acquisition of a spiritual kingship, Stephano is just a drunk. The mind of a drunkard is filled with intoxicating airs (spirits) of the wrong kind, his sight is hazy and out of focus, his thoughts are muddled and of the baser kind. He cannot even command the kingdom of his own body.

Trinculo

The name *Trinculo* seems to be one invented by Shakespeare, possibly being derived from Latin *trinus*, 'group of three', and *culleus,* 'leather bag', and certainly from *trinket,* 'a small article or ornament forming part of an outfit,' which was especially associated with a jester. *Trinket* also means 'to intrigue with or act in an underhand way'.

Trinculo is the jester or fool, whose traditional costume included a cap with asses ears and bells, together with a long sceptre or stick (called a bauble or marotte) topped by the carved head of a jester. Strung on the sceptre was a leather bag containing the fool's baubles (or trinkets), which constituted a kind of medicine bag. The jester evolved out of the once wide-spread Bardic tradition, and the jests of a well-schooled jester were equivalent to the rhyming triplets of the bards.

Caliban

Caliban is another name invented by Shakespeare to suit the purpose. Two of its derivations may be from Latin *calles,* 'thick skinned', and Hebrew *calib,* 'dog'. However, the name can easily be seen as an anagram of *Canibal* (*i.e.* Cannibal), the subject of Montaigne's essay, *Of the Canibales.*

Caliban is the bastard son of an evil witch called Sycorax and a moon spirit or god called Setebos, whom Caliban believes is the 'man in the moon'.

The name *Sycorax* is a composition of Greek *sy,* 'sow', and *corax,* 'raven', the symbolism of which implies a druidess.[15] She is described as having been banished from Argiers (Algiers) on account of her 'mischiefs manifold and sorceries terrible' (I, ii, 265-266). Because she was pregnant her life was spared. Sailors brought her to the island, where she gave birth to Caliban. She died after imprisoning Ariel in the cloven pine.

The name *Setebos* is from the Egyptian *seteb,* meaning 'what is hostile'. The Egyptians called their god of the Underworld, Set (Seth). *Set,* or *Sat,* is the root for the name of the devil, Satan, which means 'Adversary'. Setebos was mentioned in Robert Eden's *History of Travaile* (1577) as the name of the god of the Patagonians, wherein he is described as a 'great devill'.

Caliban is described as a 'salvage and deformed slave' in the 'Names of the Actors'. He is also referred to as a villain by Miranda; as earth, tortoise, poisonous slave, abhorred slave, hag-seed, malice, beast, mis-shapen knave, demi-devil and thing of darkness by Prospero; as a weak, credulous, puppy-headed, scurvy, abominable, ridiculous, howling, drunken half-fish half-monster by Trinculo; and as a man-monster, devil and moon-calf by Stephano.

Caliban is all that Ariel is not. He is fearful, whilst Ariel knows no fear. He is material, whilst Ariel is spirit. He is a creature of the water and earth elements, whilst Ariel is of the air and fire. He moves ponderously and is slow in his work, being an unwilling, grumbling worker rather than enjoying his work, as does the nimble, light-hearted Ariel. Yet Caliban can be a good helper if coaxed in the right way and if it suits him. He is primarily a creature of the senses, knowing well the elemental world of the island. He delights in the sensory world.

11. Nature's Art

The Culture of Paradise

The magical Art of Prospero is the subject of a profound philosophy that Shakespeare clearly believed in and was himself practised in, as witness the effect that his plays have on people the world over and the teachings that they convey. In connection with this, Michel de Montaigne's essay, *On Cannibals,* is of special importance.

Michel de Montaigne (1533-92) was a French lawyer, philosopher, traveller, writer and landowner from near Bordeaux, France. He composed three books of essays on various aspects of life, written from about 1572 onwards and published in 1580 and 1588. John Florio translated them into English and published them in England in 1603.

Montaigne's essays were very popular in France and highly influential, although Montaigne's observations were often far from accurate and much that he wrote is from his inventive imagination rather than observation. One of the ways in which his writings influenced people, despite the realities of the situation, were in the way voyagers to the Americas perceived the native American people. Montaigne argued for the viewpoint of an original, unblemished and perfect paradise which mankind had subsequently corrupted and spoilt; and that the American natives were savages of the primitive and innocent kind, not yet corrupted by a more civilised society. His argument was that of simple primitivism or naturalism, wherein nature left to her own devices produces fruit of admirable quality and purpose. This despite the fact that, as he notes but excuses, the natives enjoyed fighting, killing, torturing and eating each other. His excuse is that so-called civilised Europeans have often done not much better, and usually in the name of religion.

Although visitors and colonists arriving on the shores of the Americas were often met initially with friendliness, very often this amiable behaviour of the natives changed dramatically into treachery and brutality. The experienced Captain John Smith, for instance, described them as 'perfidious, inhuman, all savage,' whilst the *True Declaration* referred to them as 'human beasts'. Generally, the native American 'Indians' were found to be untrustworthy by European standards, the culture clash being enormous. Reports of the voyagers, therefore, tended to be either full of the innocence and virtue of the natives, being influenced by and supporting the thesis of Montaigne, or else damning of their vices and savagery.

Montaigne's viewpoint was not one shared by Shakespeare or anyone else connected with the Virginia Company. Mostly the Renaissance Neoplatonic and Christian viewpoint, like that of the Classical Mystery schools, supported the contrary thesis that nature, left to itself, grows wild, with certain species multiplying as weeds to devour and suffocate all others, and with the law of the jungle applying everywhere. Man, therefore, was intended to be the gardener of nature, to cultivate and help nature towards a greater expression of life and beauty, allowing all species a chance to grow to their full potential in proper balance and harmony with each other. In other words, Art improves and ultimately perfects Nature. This applies not just to the nature outside of us, in which and with which we live (*i.e.* the rocks, soil, plants, animals, birds, etc.) but our own human nature. The difficulty, of course, is in learning and applying the art of natural and social cultivation, so that there might be a paradise or golden age of wisdom, peace and prosperity on earth.

In *The Tempest* Shakespeare appears to deliberately mock the naive viewpoint of Montaigne by deliberately showing the benevolent and beneficial art of the magus in cultivating nature, controlling nature's elements and prospering the lives of others through a knowledge of and co-operation with the laws of nature.

This mastery of nature is misunderstood by a great many people. Yet it is vitally important that we should learn this art in its true sense, especially now that we are capable of mis-using our powers and resources to such an extent that we could seriously harm both humanity and nature on a vast scale. The vital point is that art is an attribute of nature, not separate from nature. That is to say, the art that masters nature is part of nature herself, but nature requires mankind to operate her art.

Francis Bacon was championing this point of view at the same time as the Shakespeare plays were being written. In 1605 he wrote that 'It is the duty of Art to perfect and exalt Nature.'[1] In 1612 he complained that it was 'the fashion to talk as if Art was something different from Nature'. In 1620 he published his famous comment on the much misunder-stood and abused Biblical declaration that man was created to have dominion over nature (Genesis i, 28): 'Nature to be commanded must be obeyed,' he said.[2] In other words, mas-tery is only obtained by service. The greatest master is the greatest servant. To be master of nature, we have to serve nature, and to serve nature we have to know and apply its highest law, which is the law of love. In 1623 he wrote:-

Still therefore it is Nature which governs everything: but under Nature are included these three; the course of Nature, the wanderings of Nature, and Art—which is Nature with man to help.[3]

In *The Winter's Tale* Shakespeare speaks openly of this same philosophy—the philosophy which pervades his plays and which gives an insight into his own art—in a conversation between Perdita and Polixenes:-

Perd.   For I have heard it said
        There is an art which in their piedness shares
        With great creating Nature.
Pol.   Say there be;
        Yet Nature is made better by no mean
        But Nature makes that mean; so over that art
        Which you say adds to Nature is an art
        That Nature makes. You see, sweet maid, we marry
        A gentler scion to the wildest stock,
        And make conceive a bark of baser kind
        By bud of nobler race. This is an art
        Which does mend Nature—change it, rather—but
        The art itself is Nature.[4]

This is culture: and natural culture is a symbol of social culture. Social culture, which is the civilising process properly applied, is a science and an art, and it requires laws and some kind of social order. Shakespeare uses Gonzalo in *The Tempest* to make his comment on this. For instance, in the Utopian musing of Gonzalo, Shakespeare deliberately paraphrases a passage from Montaigne's essay on Cannibals that offers an alternative to Plato's Ideal Republic, and presents it to the audience in a way wherein we know it to be an illusion, a false dream or foolishness, with the ideas contradicting themselves. To make this abundantly clear, Sebastian and Antonio mock the well-meaning Gonzalo:-

Gon. Had I plantation of this Isle my Lord,—
Ant. He'd sow't with nettle-seed.
Seb. Or dockes, or mallowes.
Gon. And were the King on't, what would I do?
Seb. 'Scape being drunk for want of wine.
Gon. I'th'commonwealth I would (by contraries)
    Execute all things: For no kind of traffic
    Would I admit: no name of magistrate;
    Letters should not be known; riches, poverty,
    And use of service, none; contract, succession,
    Bourn, bound of land, tilth, vineyard, none;
    No use of metal, corn, or wine, or oil;
    No occupation; all men idle, all;
    And women too, but innocent and pure:
    No sovereignty;—
Seb. Yet he would be King on't.
Ant. The latter end of his commonwealth forgets the
    beginning.
Gon. All things in common Nature should produce
    Without sweat or endeavour: treason, felony,
    Sword, pike, knife, gun, or need of any engine,
    Would I not have: but Nature should bring forth,
    Of its own kind, all foison, all abundance
    To feed my innocent people.
Seb. No marrying 'mong his subjects?
Ant. None, man, all idle; whores and knaves.
Gon. I would with such perfection govern, sir,
    T'excell the Golden Age.
Seb. 'Save his Majesty!
Ant. Long live Gonzalo! [5]

But then even Gonzalo has to admit that his speech was 'nothing' and that he was just 'fooling'.

The passage from Montaigne's essay reads as follows:-

This is a nation, I should say to Plato, that hath no kind of traffic, no knowledge of letters, no intelligence of numbers, no name of magistrate, nor of politic superiority; no use of service, of riches, or of poverty; no contracts, no successions, no partitions, no occupation, but idle; no respect of kindred, but common; no apparel, but natural; no manuring of lands; no use of wine, corn, or metal. The very words that import lying, falsehood, treason, dissimulation, covetousness, envy, detraction, and pardon, were never heard amongst them.[6]

Montaigne was influenced no doubt by the legends of the golden age of Atlantis. In his *Cannibals* essay he refers to both Plato's description of Atlantis and Aristotle's supposed story about Carthage and the Carthaginians, relating the stories again in his own words and with his own embellishments. About the Carthaginians he says:-

The other testimonie of antiquitie, to which some will referre this discoverie, is in Aristotle (if at least that little booke of unheard of wonders be his), where he reporteth that certaine Carthaginans having sailed athwart the Atlantike Sea, without the strait of Gibraltar, after long time, they at last discovered a great fertill Iland, all replenished with goodly woods, and watred with great and deepe rivers, farre distant from al land, and that both they and others, allured by the goodnes and fertility of the soile, went thither with their wives, children and household, and there began to inhabit and settle themselves. The Lords of Carthage seeing their countrie by little and little to be dispeopled, made a law and expresse inhibition, that upon paine of death no more men should goe thither, and banished all that were gone thither to dwell, fearing (as they said) that in success of time, they would so multiply as they might one day supplant them, and overthrow their owne estate. This narration of Aristotle hath no reference unto our new found countries.[7]

By making Gonzalo a kind of alter ego of Montaigne,

with a clear reference to the *Cannibals* essay, Shakespeare is able to contrast the well-meaning but naïve simplicity and ignorance of Montaigne's *laissez faire* policy with the high magical art of Prospero that is in effect a science of love and charity.

The main point made in *The Tempest* is that love, consciously, wisely and justly applied, is the art that masters nature, human and otherwise. Moreover, one must do this as a servant of nature, and thereby unlock and release the love that is not only in our hearts but also in the heart of all nature—even in the very atoms of matter.

This Thing of Darkness

The biggest test confronting Prospero is Caliban's nature. Prospero refers to Caliban as 'thou earth' and 'this thing of he human characters in *The Tempest*, Caliban portrays the most complete polarity to Prospero. Prospero is seen by Caliban (eventually) as the master and god for whom he (Caliban) has been seeking, whilst Caliban is seen by Prospero as a 'born devil'. Prospero is the magus of light; Caliban is the 'thing of darkness'. Prospero is philosophical, highly educated, disciplined, virtuous, refined in his manners, loving as a father and humane as a person. He is by virtue of his greater attainments and magic the ruler of the island, and the judge and lawmaker. He is responsible for creating and maintaining peace, justice and harmony in his kingdom. Caliban, by contrast, is none of these things, but is a brutish, deformed creature, half-fish, half-man, crude, lecherous, savage, dangerous, and seemingly incapable of education and the finer things of life, despite Prospero's love and care put into teaching him. He uses the language he has been taught to curse ('You taught me language; and my profit on't is, I know how to curse.' – I, ii, 365-366), and abuses Prospero and Miranda's trust by attempting to rape Miranda.

Prospero, who tried and seemingly failed to civilise Caliban, seems at the start of the play to have given up trying any further. He berates Caliban as the bastard son of a witch who dealt in evil things, not good, implying that evil runs in Caliban's blood and always will. But this is a dangerous assumption, based on the ancient belief that evil is passed on from parents to children, including the misunderstood and misapplied dogma concerning original sin. It leaves no room for either innocence or redemption.[8] Also, Prospero has over-looked that Caliban did learn how to speak, and doesn't always use his words to curse. As the play reveals, when Stephano and Trinculo appear, Caliban is only too ready to serve them as best he might—although at the same time he does incite them to attempt to kill Prospero and make a whore out of Miranda. Miranda exclaims that Caliban is an 'abhorred slave, which any print of goodness wilt not take, being capable of all ill' (I, ii, 353-355). Her words, echoing Bacon's expression that 'truth prints goodness',[9] imply that it is impossible for truth (*i.e.* love) to make any impression on Caliban, or for him to express that truth in any goodness of nature. But in fact every person alive is potentially capable of all ill. It is only through the development of our moral natures, through love, self-discipline, goodwill, right effort, and example, that we don't lapse into evil. This comprises an education.

> …The other [force] is that noble thing call'd *Education*, this is, that Harp of *Orpheus*, that lute of *Amphion*, so elegantly figur'd by the Poets to have wrought such Miracles among irrational and insensible Creatures, which raiseth beauty even out of deformity, order and regularity out of Chaos and confusion, and which, if thoroughly and rightly pros-ecuted, would be able to civilize the most savage natures, & root out barbarism and ignorance from off the face of

the Earth: those who have either of these qualifications singly may justly be term'd *Men*; those who have both united in a happy conjunction, *more* than *Men*; those who have neither of them in any competent measure...*less* than *Men*...[10]

In his essay Montaigne chiefly writes of the savage nature of certain cannibalistic tribes encountered in America, but Shakespeare makes it more universal, as a nature applicable to all people if not controlled, tamed and transmuted. Shakespeare does this by linking the name of Caliban to the Americas *via* Montaigne's essay on Cannibals, whilst at the same time stating that Caliban was the bastard son of the evil witch Sycorax, who came from Algiers, and the moon-god Setebos (the 'man in the moon').

Algiers, like Tunisia, is situated in northwest Africa, inhabited traditionally by black or dark-skinned people. Northwest Africa used to be known as Barbary to the Europeans, on account of it being the home of the Berbers (Saracens), who were fervent Muslims. Christians regarded it therefore, as a heathen country. In that sense *Barbary* referred to foreign nationality and heathenism, or non-Christianity. Due to ignorance, prejudice, and political and religious intolerance, the word became the root of *barbarity*, in the sense of not just uncivilised manners and culture but uncultivated speech in particular. This barbarity is portrayed as the primary nature of Caliban.

In the language of symbolism (as distinct from historical truth), the black or dark colour commonly represents ignorance, barbarity, savagery, vice and the devil: in fact, all that into which we, as a human race, fell when cast out of our original paradisiacal state of innocence. This darkness or 'hell' is also associated with the lower area of the body and the functions of sex, sensation, sensuality, sluggishness, ego-power, self-preservation, food, drink, selfishness, etc.. These are all basic, and some of them are base, functions in the human being, and we all possess them; but they are only a part of us. Whether we like them or not, these functions are necessary to us, but they should not rule us. They relate to what we usually call the mundane or servile jobs that have to be carried out, and which those people with jobs of a more intellectual (*i.e.* head) nature tend to despise and undervalue. Prospero is quite clear about this, when he addresses Miranda's abhorrence of Caliban:-

> *Mir.*   'Tis a villain, sir,
>   I do not love to look on.
> *Pros.*   But as 'tis,
>   We cannot miss him: he does make our fire,
>   Fetch in our wood, and serves in offices
>   That profit us.[11]

The Greeks and Egyptians referred to the abdomen area of the body, with its functions and associations, as the underworld, relating by correspondence to the terrestrial world of the elements. Whilst the Greeks saw this realm as ruled over by Hades, the Egyptians called the god of the underworld Set (Seth), a name which is associated with the root of Setebos, Caliban's spirit father (from Egyptian *seteb*, 'what is hostile'). Since *Set* is the root for the name *Satan* (*i.e.* 'the hostile one' or 'Adversary'), Robert Eden accurately describes Setebos as a 'great devill' in his *History of Travaile*: for Seth/Hades became known in Christianity as the Devil (Satan) and the underworld as hell.[12]

The Egyptians symbolised Set as a snake, who is killed, eaten and thereby transformed into a better nature by Horus, whose symbolical form is a hawk. This allegory and symbolism translates into Christianity as the story of St George (or St Michael) and the dragon, which Spenser portrayed as the

Red Cross knight and the dragon in his *Faerie Queene*. In addition, Hebraic and Christian tradition used the symbolism of the sea-monster for the Devil. Then, using Orphic symbolism, the sea-monster becomes a fish (*i.e.* a disciple) through purification, education and discipline. When ready, the fish is then speared (or netted) and lifted out of the sea by the Great Fisherman, cooked upon the fire of the Holy Spirit and eaten, thereby becoming part of the mystical body of Christ.[13] The Christian Church today still retains this symbolism in the mitre and crosier of the bishop—the mitre representing a fish head, and the crosier being a compound of a shepherd's crook and a fisherman's spear. The spear, whether wielded by Orpheus, Christ, St Michael, St George, St Margaret, Apollo or Pallas Athena, symbolises the ray of love-light, of wisdom and mercy, and is traditionally known as the 'shaking spear'—'shaking' because it is vibrating with light and the creative sound of love-wisdom. Hence the name *Shake-speare* is an immensely suitable name for the author of plays dealing with Nature's Art—the Art of the Magus.

Heaven is the abode of God; hell is the realm of the Devil. The one is light, the other dark: the one is spiritual, the other material. They are natural polarities to each other, the Devil being the opposite in nature to God. This is cryptically referred to in the use of the word *dog*, for DOG is GOD spelt backwards. It is no wonder, therefore, to discover that Shakespeare has used the Hebrew word *calib*, meaning 'dog', as a root for *Caliban*. In this Shakespeare gives us a key. The key is to love one's dog. Tamed, loved and treated well, the dog can become a man's best friend; but mistreated or left wild, the dog can be savage and dangerous, even man-eating, as many people have learnt to their horror.

> For take an example of a dog, and mark what a generosity and courage he will put on when he finds himself main-

tained by a man, who to him is in stead of a god, or *melior natura*; which courage is manifestly such as that creature, without that confidence of a better nature than his own, could never attain.[14]

Merlin is always accompanied by his black dog. Likewise the man in the moon is always accompanied by his dog. Setebos is described as the god of the moon, and Caliban saw him as the man in the moon; but in reality Setebos is the dog aspect rather than the god aspect, the brute soul rather than the spiritual soul. Referring to Setebos and the moon, Caliban says:-

> *Cal.*   I have seen thee in her, and I do adore thee:
> My mistress show'd me thee, and thy dog, and thy bush.[15]

The Rosicrucians were referred to as the 'men in the moon' by Ben Jonson, and it is Prospero himself, the Phoenix or Rosicrucian, who is the real moon-god. He is the one who can control Setebos and, therefore, Caliban: but he has to learn how to do this proficiently, step by step. Referring to Prospero, Caliban says:-

> *Cal.*   I must obey: his Art is of such pow'r,
> It would control my dam's god, Setebos,
> And make a vassal of him.[16]

Caliban shows himself as looking for his father, hoping to find his 'god' whom he might worship. In his eagerness he readily mistakes the drunken Stephano for his father-god. But the spiritual father whom Caliban really longs for, without yet realising it, is the real man in the moon, not the dog.

The character list of *The Tempest* deliberately describes Caliban as a 'salvage' rather than a savage, and this would appear to be a clever way of conveying not only the idea of a savage nature but also one that can be and is being salvaged. It brings to mind the teachings concerning Orpheus, who could move mountains and tame the wild beasts by the sound of his music, especially since Caliban himself makes mention of the beautiful soothing music of the isle:-

> *Cal.*   Be not afeard; the isle is full of noises,
> Sounds and sweet airs, that give delight, and hurt not.
> Sometimes a thousand twangling instruments
> Will hum about mine ears; and sometimes voices,
> That, if I had wak'd after long sleep,
> Will make me sleep again: and then, in dreaming,
> The clouds methought would open, and show riches
> Ready to drop on me; that, when I wak'd,
> I cried to dream again.[17]

Caliban is related very strongly to the water element throughout the play. For instance, he is referred to as a fish, a tortoise and a monster. These are descriptions of the three water signs in the Zodiac: Pisces (symbolised by two fishes tied together), Cancer (symbolised by a crab or tortoise) and Scorpio (symbolised by a scorpion or sea monster). The 'monster' appellation is emphasised more than any other description of Caliban, with reason, for Scorpio is the sign of both death and regeneration.

The sting in the tail of the scorpion is renowned for inflicting the deathblow; yet it is out of death that new life is born, wherein the initiate is resurrected as the adept, and the adept is exalted as the master. Caliban's desire to kill Prospero is exactly of this nature, and Caliban has a tail for the job, yet he dares not kill Prospero unaided.

Scorpio contains the mystery of the deepest darkness, the profoundest depths of the subconscious containing the sludge and the monstrous, fearsome things of darkness that dwell in the recesses of the psyche. But the adept knows that this sludge and dark ugliness is but the material given to him to work upon, like a potter working with clay, in order to create yet more shining beauty. Hence the sign of Scorpio has other images associated with it that represent higher stages of evolution—namely, a serpent, an eagle and a dove. The earthly scorpion can become a sea-monster or serpent, the serpent can become the far-sighted eagle soaring in the air towards the sun, and the eagle can become the phoenix-dove, descending in a halo-fire of love to bring peace to the world.

Therefore, perhaps the highest and most moving moment of the play is near the end, when Caliban sees Prospero with new eyes and exclaims, 'How fine my Master is!'—And Prospero acknowledges Caliban as his own, adopting him as a son and recognising him as part of himself, not separate. Having now discovered his true god-father, Caliban vows:-

> *Cal.* … and I'll be wise hereafter,
>   And seek for grace: what a thrice-double ass
>   Was I to take this drunkard [Stephano] for a god,
>   And worship this dull fool [Trinculo].[18]

To accept and work with in love, but not suppress, the lower instincts and desires, without losing virtue or discipline, is not easy. To give up one's hard-earned mental powers of control, and become humble, relying totally on love, whilst at the same time steadily educating and transmuting the lower self by means of that love, is tricky. But when it can be truly done, mastery is attained. The Rosicrucians describe this as the humbling of Aries to become the sacrificial Lamb, and the raising of Scorpio to become the Eagle. The story of *The Tempest* is a portrayal of this great Mystery, this great Art of Nature.

12. The Rosicrucians

The Art of Prospero is very much the Rosicrucian Art. This Art is the skilful ability to put good, loving thought into action as charity. As specified by Bacon, the Rosicrucian Master, such thought is to embrace matters divine, human and natural, is to be inspired and guided by Divinity, is to be well tested according to an experimental method, and is to be put into action in both mechanical and magical ways for the good of all. The mechanical operations relate to physics, involving the laws of the physical universe. The magical operations relate to metaphysics, involving the laws of the psyche and spirit—the ultimate law being love.

The story of Prospero is the story of a Rosicrucian adept practising what he has learnt at a fairly high level, enabling him to control not only the natural elements but to be a powerful teacher of human ethics and both judge and initiator of others. Having worked on himself in the crucible of the island, he brings other people, other human souls, through transformative experiences according to and by means of the laws of nature, as was done from ancient times by the adepts in the Mystery schools, purifying and raising their souls to a higher level of life and behaviour. He does not know all, however, and so he quite rightly learns more and more as he goes along concerning the supreme law of love, until ultimately he is ready to work completely with that supreme law, giving up his reliance on the lesser laws and setting love totally free from within himself to do its creative work. He becomes, at the end of the play, not just an adept but also a potential master, needing but our 'indulgence' and recognition to complete his initiation. '*Liber Bacchus!*'—'Bacchus the Free!'—was the cry of recognition in the Classical Mystery schools as each new Bacchus was born. 'Free' means 'love' and indicates the state of a master.

The Duke of Milan

This link with the Rosicrucians and with Rosicrucian philosophy has been made very deliberately by Shakespeare, not only by portraying an example of a Rosicrucian in the character of Prospero but by the use of the history of Ludovic Sforza, Duke of Milan, as a source for his story of Prospero. This Milanese history has a close association with the Rosicrucian manifestos which were being circulated in manuscript at the same time as the last Shakespeare plays being written and given their first performances.

The history of Ludovic Sforza is given in the *Treasury of Ancient and Modern Times*, as translated out of the Spanish of Pedro Mexia and Francesco Sansovino, and published in London by John Jaggard in 1613-19. The history commences as follows:-

> Ludovic Sforza was brother to Galeas Sforza, duke of Milan, named by some John Andrea, whom he nourished and brought up, and slew in the church of St Stephen, in Milan, as he was there present at the hearing of mass, albeit they were both sons of the famous warrior, Francis Sforza. By the death of Galeas, a son of his named John, very young in years, remained his successor in the tutelage of Bona, his mother, and of Chico, a native of Calabria, who had been much favoured by his father and

grandfather. This Chico immediately banished Ludovic, who wandered as a fugitive through strange countries, and tasted the mutabilities of fortune.

The history continues with an account of Ludovic returning from his banishment and forcibly entering Milan. Having expelled Bona and Chico he then ruled Milan for the next twenty years with great wisdom and spirit. He married his nephew, the Duke Ferdinand, to the King of Naples' daughter.

In this history we can see a basis of the plot in *The Tempest*, twisted somewhat but still eminently recognisable. We have two brothers, one of whom usurps the position of duke of Milan from his elder brother. We have the banishment of a duke of Milan, followed by his wanderings abroad through strange lands and his tasting of the 'mutabilities of fortune', through the experience of which he undoubtedly learnt the wisdom with which he was later able to rule Milan. We have a restoration of this duke to his dukedom, howbeit forcibly. We have a councillor who was much favoured by the father of the young duke, and who cared for and helped to educate the young nobleman. Furthermore we have a Ferdinand and a king of Naples whose daughter Ferdinand marries, thereby cementing an alliance between Naples and Milan. Shakespeare switches some of the roles of the characters, but the history of Prospero is clearly analogous to this history of Ludovic.

The Rosicrucian association is provided by a neat little treasure trail. The father of Ludovic and Galeas is named as the famous warrior, Francis Sforza. We find this same famous gentleman mentioned in the 53rd Advertisement of the *Ragguagli di Parnasso* ('News from Parnassus'), volume 1, written by Trajano Boccalini and published at Venice in 1612:-

> Apollo at last grants admittance into Parnassus to Francisco Sforza, Duke of Milan, which he had long

denied to do, upon a hard condition, which he accepted of.

The symbolism of the Rosicrucian allegories is largely based upon the Classical symbolism of Apollo and Athena, their two sons Æsculapius and Dionysus, and their home of Mount Parnassus, on which once rested the Ark of Deucalion after the Great Flood which destroyed the former world. On the slopes of this mountain of poetic inspiration and illumination, sacred to the Muses, the Delphic Oracle was founded.[1]

The first Rosicrucian manifesto, the *Fama Fraternitatis*, published in 1614, is deliberately placed after a 'light' story concerning Apollo. This story is none other than the 77th Advertisement of Boccalini's *Ragguagli di Parnasso*. This 77th Advertisement, entitled *The General and Universal Reformation of the Whole World*, supplies the main title of the 1614 manifesto publication and the bulk (approximately two-thirds) of its contents.

The 77th Advertisement is a jest in satirical vein, relating how Apollo, greatly concerned to hear that human affairs had come to such a dreadful state, determined to cure the world and, for that purpose, to found a society of men famous for wisdom and virtue who could carry out the required reformation. However, this proved difficult, for he was unable to discover a single person who possessed even one-half of the qualifications required. Finally Apollo decided to leave the reformation of the world in charge of the Seven Wise Men of Greece, plus two Latins (Seneca and Cato) and an Italian (Jacapo Mazzoni da Cesena) whom he made Secretary. The end result was that none of them were able to succeed. Moreover, becoming confused by all their various and conflicting proposals, despairing of doing anything sufficient for the purpose, and looking into the future and discerning the present age to be thoroughly corrupt and ailing, they forthwith abandoned the world as incurable and took to providing for their own safety.

Nevertheless, one of the sages, Solon, comes near the mark when he notes that what the world really needs is not so much a reform of society as more human love, charity and affection. How to generate such love and apply it is the problem.

This satire is then followed by the *Fama Fraternitatis*, which proceeds to bring things up to date, declaring that, thanks to the 'only Wise and Merciful God' who 'in these latter days hath poured out his mercy and goodness to Mankind, whereby we do attain more and more to the perfect knowledge of his Son Jesus Christ and *Nature*', men had been raised 'indued with great wisdom, which might partly renew and reduce all Arts...to perfection, so that finally Man might thereby understand his own Nobleness and Worth, and why he is called *Microsomus*, and how far his knowledge extendeth in Nature'. Thanks to their Father, Fra. C. R. C., who had laboured long and hard to bring the learned of all nations together in unity of thought and purpose, and to prepare for a General Reformation of the world, certain of these wise ones had been brought together in fellowship by their Father and been given by him a 'perfect Method of all Arts' by means of which to cleanse and reform the world. This fellowship of the wise was known as 'the Fraternity of the Rosie Cross', all of whom were 'betrothed to wisdom' (*i.e.* philosophers in the highest sense), and they had begun the General and Universal Reformation of the whole wide world in earnest, but anonymously, in disguise—which reminds us of the words of Jaques in *As You Like It*:-

> Invest me in my motley. Give me leave
> To speak my mind, and I will through and through
> Cleanse the foul body of th'infected world,
> If they will patiently receive my medicine.[2]

The Rosicrucian Manifestos
& Johann Valentine Andreæ

The Rosicrucian manifestos, of which the *Fama* was the first, began to be published soon after the Palatinate Elector, Frederick, and King James' daughter, Princess Elizabeth, had taken up residence in Heidelberg after their London wedding in 1613, at which *The Tempest* had been performed. During the next seven years, whilst the manifestos were being published in Germany and elsewhere, the couple made Heidelberg castle into a remarkable centre of advanced culture, science and learning such as promulgated by the Rosicrucians and outlined in Francis Bacon's scheme (The Great Instauration) for the advancement and proficience of learning.

Having been in circulation in manuscript form since at least 1610 (but not earlier than 1604), the *Fama Fraternitatis* or *A Discovery of the Fraternity of the Most Noble Order of the Rosy Cross*, was published in German at Cassel in 1614. It encouraged the advancement of learning and was introduced by the above-mentioned tract (the 77th Advertisement) declaring a 'Universal and General Reformation of the whole wide world'. It was quickly followed by its sequel, the *Confessio Fraternitatis* or *The Confession of the Laudable Fraternity of the Most Honourable Order of the Rosy Cross, Written to All the Learned of Europe*, published in Latin at Cassel in 1615.

Each manifesto had a *Preface*, and in addition was bound with certain other texts and letters which helped to elucidate the message of the manifestos. Thus, bound with the *Fama* and preceding it, was the *Allgemeine und General Reformation* ('The Universal and General Reformation'), a German translation of an extract from Traiano Boccalini's *Ragguagli di Parnaso*. The *Confessio* was prefixed with the *Secretioris Philosophiae Consideratio brevis* ('A Brief Consideration of the more Secret Philosophy') by Philip à Gabella. This latter was based upon (and much of it quoted from) Dr. John Dee's *Monas Hieroglyphica,* and identifies Dee's philosophy, as summed up in the *Monas,* as being at the root of the Rosicrucian manifestos.[3] Other editions followed, with further insertions and some rewriting. An *Assertio* was included in the 1616 edition (the tenth edition), and an important postscript in the form of a *Report concerning a great secret of Nature* was added in the final edition of 1617. The *Fama, Confessio, Assertio* and *Report,* together with the two Prefaces, comprised the authentic Rosicrucian manifestos: the rest were simply embellishments included to be helpful.

Like *The Tempest* and the rest of the Shakespeare plays and poems, the Rosicrucian manifestos provide what is basically an allegorical story—a *'ludibrium'* or 'jest', as the German Lutheran pastor and theologian, Johann Valentine Andreæ, meaningfully remarked about them. However, a jest is no nonsense—as Jaques, who wishes to be a court jester, makes clear in *As You Like It* (see quote above).

The manifestos describe the mythical history of the fabled Fra. C.R.C., the 'Father' of the Rosicrucian fraternity, the cipher of whom some interpret as 'Brother Christian Rosie Cross' and others as 'Francis Rosicross',[4] and whom the Order Kabbalistique de la Rose Croix of 1891 identified as the 'Spirit of Liberty, of Science and Love, which must regenerate the world'.

Like *The Tempest*, the Rosicrucian manifestos are constructed on Hermetic-Cabalistic foundations, and describe the work of Fra. C.R.C. and the Rosicrucian fraternity as the great Art of illuminating the mind and doing good in the world. To those with no knowledge of the Cabala or the Hermetic sciences, the allegorical symbolism and ciphers in the manifestos would almost certainly never be recognised and the deeper significance of the story would be

7. TITLE PAGE OF DR JOHN DEE'S MONAS HIEROGLYPHICA (1564)

Depicting the mercurial Monas Hieroglyphica set in its cosmic egg
between the Twin Pillars of Sun and Moon.

**8. Title page of Francis Bacon's *Novum Organum*,
'The Great Instauration' (1620)**

Depicting the two Great Pillars or Pillars of Hercules.

misunderstood; but in the late Renaissance period the study of Cabala and the Hermetic sciences by the intelligentsia of that time was relatively more common than nowadays and thus more likely to be perceived and understood, howbeit in varying degrees.[5] The manifestos formed, therefore, an exciting treasure hunt for those so inclined, and a gateway to the real world of the Rosicrucians.

The four Rosicrucian manifestos (the *Fama*, *Confessio*, *Assertio* and *Report*), plus the two different editions of the *Fama*'s Preface, were clearly not the work of one man. As noted by scholars, the first *Report* and the *Assertio* markedly differ from each other and from the *Fama* and *Confessio*.[6] It is possible that the *Fama* and *Confessio*, in their final forms, were written by the same person, but not initially—the first edition of the *Fama* showing signs of having been reworked by the author of the *Confessio*, the latter also probably being the author of the second *Preface* but not the first. The evidence suggests the co-operation of at least four people in the authorship, and a further two or more in the translations. Moreover, the influence on the manifestos of the English magus, Dr. John Dee, is apparent; whilst the principal Rosicrucian theme of the advancement of learning and reformation of the world through the regeneration of the arts and sciences, and the forming of a fraternity in learning to accomplish this, is identical with the Great Instauration of Dee's successor, Sir Francis Bacon.

However, the impression was allowed to grow that Johann Valentine Andreæ was the author of at least the *Fama* if not the *Confessio*, despite his own denials of this. In the history of Ludovic Sforza the name of John Andrea is peculiarly introduced as a name for Galeas Sforza, the Duke of Milan who was slain by his brother (see above).

Andreæ wrote several books, including *Chymishe Hochzeit Christiani Rosenkreutz* ('The Chemical Wedding of

Christian Rosicross', published in 1616), *Invitatio Fraternitatis Christianæ* ('Invitation to a Christian Fraternity', published in 1617), *Mythologiæ Christianæ Libri tres* ('Three Books of Christian Mythology', published in 1918) and *Reipublicæ Christianopolitanæ Descriptio* ('Description of the Republic of Christianopolis', published in 1619).

The *Chemical Wedding* is an alchemical allegory in which Andreæ contributes to the *ludibrium* of the Rosicrucians. It shows signs of having been strongly influenced by the English plays and investiture of the Duke of Württemberg with the Order of the Garter in 1604 (which Andreæ witnessed at Tübingen), by the marriage of Frederick and Elizabeth in 1613 and their Baconian-Rosicrucian-type activities at Heidelberg Castle, and by the philosophy of Dee— even to the extent of showing the hieroglyphic Monad of Dee's near the beginning of the *Chemical Marriage.*

Like Shakespeare's *Tempest*, the *Chemical Wedding* commences with a tempest theme and concludes with ships sailing safely away after instruction and alchemical initiation; but in Andreæ's romance the hero of the story is clearly identified as a Brother of the Rosy Cross.

Also showing links with Shakespeare's *Tempest*, Andreæ's *Christianopolis* likewise begins with a tempest and a shipwreck; and those who are shipwrecked are cast upon an island containing the ideal city of Christianopolis which is governed by a Society of Christian philosopher-scientists—a theme which is practically identical with Bacon's *New Atlantis* and which emphasises the Baconian principle of conjoining divinity with philosophy, and science (speculative thought) with art (practical operation). Andreæ called this 'theosophy'. Another Rosicrucian apologist, Theophilus Schweighardt, referred to it as 'Pansophia',[7] thereby providing another key, for the great god Pan (whose name means 'the All') is identical to Saturn or Cronos, the lord of time and space, and ruler of the Blessed Isles. Pansophia, or theosophy, is entirely the science and art of Prospero in *The Tempest*, who rules his island as a Cronos figure and, like Cronos or Time, brings forth truth.

Instead of claiming authorship of the Rosicrucian manifestos, which he readily did for the works which were genuinely his own, by 1619 Andreæ was deliberately distancing himself from the Rosicrucian furore which had been aroused, emphasising that the Rosicrucian manifestos had been but a *ludibrium* or 'comedy', misinterpreted by many people, and that the Rosicrucian Fraternity were 'an admirable Fraternity which plays comedies throughout Europe'.[8] In his *Christian Mythology* he implies that he approved of and thoroughly enjoyed the 'play', of which he was neither the author nor an actor but a 'spectator'.

Prospero Colonna

The entry into the treasure trail is completed by the reference in Boccalini's *Ragguagli di Parnasso* to a certain historical gentleman, Prospero Colonna, who is admitted into Parnassus on account of his extraordinary virtues and literary acquirements. The meaning of the name Prospero has already been discussed (see Chapter 10), but its link with Colonna, emphasised by its inclusion in Boccalini's book and the deliberate allegorical association of both names with someone who is able to be admitted into the Mountain or Temple of Light on account of his extraordinary virtues and literary acquirements, should be noted. Such a person who achieves this is an adept, a magus, which is exactly what is portrayed for us by the character of Prospero in *The Tempest*.

The name *Colonna* is significant in that it leads us straight to certain signatures or ciphers used in the various interrelated 'Rosicrucian' works of the European Mystery School. One instance of this, which is relevant to Prospero in *The Tempest*, is that Christopher Columbus usually signed himself 'Colon'.

Columbus is famed for his 'discovery' of the Americas, which led to the colonisation of the vast continent by European settlers, fortune seekers, and some who sought to build there a just and free society of mixed races and enlightened democracy. What is not so well known is that 'Christopher Columbus' was a pseudonym adopted by a man well educated in the classics and of impressive personality, who had travelled extensively and who had (according to his own report) 'endeavoured to see all books of cosmography, history and philosophy and of other sciences', who was probably Greek (according to his son and others)—perhaps even Prince Nikolaos Ypsilantis—and who seems to have had links with members of certain secret societies of the European Mystery School that culminated at the end of the Renaissance with the Rosicrucians and their new and perfect Method of all Arts. For many centuries these secret societies had been preparing for the time when the European colonisation of the Americas ('the continent of Atlantis') could occur, and the meeting of the white race with the red race take place; thereby fulfilling the prophecy known on both sides of the Atlantic by the sages of both races, that when the white and the red races come together again in brotherhood then the Golden Age will begin.

Furthermore, Columbus is associated symbolically with the name of Francis, via the Franciscan Order founded by St Francis of Assisi. Columbus is recorded as having often dressed in a plain robe and girdle similar to the costume of the Franciscan Order, and his son reported that his father died wearing a Franciscan frock. In the Shakespeare plays the Franciscans feature over and over again, offering down-to-earth, practical yet spiritual advice and help, and appearing as wise, humble, caring brothers dedicated to love, science and charity. They may well be intended as symbolic examples of the 'invisible' Rosicrucian brethren, especially as 'Francis' means 'Free' and 'free' is the final word and signature of *The Tempest*. One of the most famous Franciscans was the mage Roger Bacon who was, like Prospero, reputed for both his learning and magic, and imprisoned for a time as a result.

The Double A

In the story of *The Tempest*, Milan is significant, as also is Naples. As already mentioned, Milan was once a second Athens, founded with a boar (or sow) sacrifice and famed for its arts and sciences. Naples was the capital of the kingdom of Naples, founded by the Greek Chalcideans of Cumae and famed for its beauty. Prospero, like the Francis Svorza who gained admittance into Parnassus, is the Duke of Milan. Alonso is king of Naples, and his son Ferdinand is his heir. Prospero's daughter, Miranda, the bride of Ferdinand, will one day become queen of Naples. This leads us to another literary treasure trail, associated with the first.

In a certain book of emblems assembled and produced under the name of the Milanese sage, Andreas Alciat, a symbolic key to the link between Naples, Milan, London, the Rosicrucians, Freemasonry, Shakespeare, and the Ancient Mysteries and Gnosis may be found. The book, Alciat's *Emblemata*, was first published in 1546 and reprinted several times during the succeeding four decades, each time with certain meaningful alterations. The symbolic key is the 'Double A' ('AA') device, which was used in the form of an ornamental headpiece that heads the dedication page of *Venus and Adonis*, the learned but sensuous poem which in 1593 announced Shakespeare to the world for the first time. Besides being used in several Shakespeare quartos and various books by Bacon, Jonson, Spenser and other authors, the device was employed again in the 1623 Shakespeare Folio, in a differently designed headpiece that blatantly alludes to the Classical and Freemasonic Mysteries.

The 'A' is the Alpha (Hebrew *Aleph*), symbol of the Beginning and the Creator, the Word or Wisdom of God. The second 'A', which is often shown in shadow, signifies the polarity, either as the Omega, the End, and that which is Created, or as the Divine Intelligence or Holy Ghost which is the receptacle, bearer and revealer of the Word. The 'Double A' thus represents the Divine Father and Mother, the primordial and archetypal Male and Female. In terms of human knowledge and illumination, the 'Double A' also signifies Apollo and Athena, or Apollo and Artemis.

In this literary treasure hunt it is, of course, significant that Andreas Alciat's initials are 'AA'. Valentine Andreæ's initials, 'VA', have a similar connotation, the 'V' being an inverted 'A', the mirror image or receptacle ('grail') of the 'A'. The initials of both persons represent two triangles which, when conjoined, render the Seal of Solomon. When the two triangles become fully 'married', this Seal shines with light and becomes the six-pointed Star of David or Christ Star, the sign of the Master. This Star is known in Freemasonry as the Blazing Star and is used particularly in Royal Arch Masonry. It signifies the crown of all endeavour, and for this reason it is used as the symbol of the North Pole Star, the guiding light centred above the crown of the earth and our heads.

The profound symbolism of Solomon's Seal is such that the upward-pointing triangle signifies spiritual Fire, the Divine Wisdom or 'Father', represented by the Hebrew letter *Shin* ('Sh') or word *Chamah*. The downward-pointing triangle signifies spiritual Water, the Holy Intelligence or 'Mother', represented by the Hebrew letter *Mem* ('M') or word *Majim*. The two triangles conjoined signify Æther, the spiritual Air or

TO THE RIGHT HONORABLE
Henrie VVriothesly, Earle of Southampton,
and Baron of Titchfield.

*Ight Honourable , I know not how I shall offend in
dedicating my vnpolisht lines to your Lordship,
nor how the vvorld vvill censure me for choosing
so strong a proppe to support so vveake a burthen,
onely if your Honour seeme but pleased , I account
my selfe highlie praysed, and vow to take aduantage of all idle
boures , till I haue honoured you vvith some grauer labour . But
if the first heyre of my inuention proue deformed, I shall be sory it
had so noble a god-father : and neuer after eare so barren a land,
for feare it yeeld me still so bad a harueft , I leaue it to your Honourable furuey, and your Honor to your hearts content, vvhich I wish
may alwayes anfwere your owne vvish, and the vvorlds hopefull
expectation.*

Your Honors in all dutie,

William Shakefpeare.

9. DEDICATION PAGE OF SHAKESPEARE'S *VENUS AND ADONIS* (1593)
The page is headed by a 'Double A' headpiece.

Vpon the Lines and Life of the Famous
Scenicke Poet, Maſter WILLIAM
SHAKESPEARE.

THoſe hands, which you ſo clapt, go now, and wring
You *Britaines* braue; for done are *Shakeſpeares* dayes :
His dayes are done, that made the dainty Playes,
Which made the Globe of heau'n and earth to ring.
Dry'de is that veine, dry'd is the *Theſpian* Spring,
Turn'd all to teares, and *Phœbus* clouds his rayes :
That corp's, that coffin now beſticke thoſe bayes,
Which crown'd him *Poet* firſt, then *Poets* King.
If *Tragedies* might any *Prologue* haue,
All thoſe he made, would ſcarſe make one to this :
Where *Fame*, now that he gone is to the graue
(Deaths publique tyring-houſe) the *Nuncius* is.
    For though his line of life went ſoone about,
    The life yet of his lines ſhall neuer out.

HVGH HOLLAND.

10. TRIBUTARY PAGE, 'UPON THE LINES AND LIFE OF …

WILLIAM SHAKESPEARE', SHAKESPEARE FOLIO (1623).

The page is headed by a 'Double A' headpiece.

Mercury, represented by the Hebrew letter *Aleph* ('A') and the word *Shamaim*, compounded of *Shin* and *Mem*. This is the 'Son' or Light of Love, *Chiram*, whose name is derived from the first letters of *Chamah*, *Ruach* and *Majim*. (See Chapter 4, 'Ariel: Hiram Abif'.)

Although the symbolism is very ancient, the earliest date at which the 'Double A' seems to have appeared in print is in 1563. It appears in the form of an emblematic headpiece to John Baptista Porta's cipher book, *De Furtivis Literarum Notis, Vulgo De Ziferis,* printed in Naples. From Naples the emblem emigrated, as it were, to Milan, to be included in a 1577 edition of Andreas Alciat's *Emblemata*, published by Christopher Plantin in Antwerp. Significantly, Andreas Alciatus, or Alciat, who was born in Milan, was described by De Bry as being not only 'the most noble jurisconsult, but in all liberal learning, and especially poetry, so experienced that he could vie with the very highest geniuses'.[9] Shakespeare's Prospero, who certainly acts as a noble jurisconsult and judge, and who describes himself as 'the prime duke, being so reputed in dignity, and for the liberal Arts without a parallel' (I, ii, 70-74), seems to be intentionally a second Andreas Alciat.

The 'Double A' appears in Plantin's 1577 edition in an entirely new emblem, No. XLV, which for some reason was introduced in place of the original emblem as published in the Aldine 'Fountain' edition of 1546. This new emblem depicts a boar rooting the ground, with a swineherd standing by it, pointing with his left hand at the boar and his right hand at the two pillars of a ruined temple which are left standing solitarily above its crypt. Wrapped around and between these twin pillars is a banner displaying the motto *'Plus Oltra'*. Then, running along and above the spine of the boar is another motto, *'Ulterius'*. When the two mottoes are read together with the symbolism of the pointing swineherd, the picture can be understood as giving an exhortation to the viewer to go further, to go beyond the two pillars. This is a most perfect Freemasonic emblem, alluding to the ruined Temple of Solomon with its Great Pillars that remained standing on top of the underfloor crypt, and to the Royal Arch Degree in which the Lost Word is found and raised up from the deepest underground crypt of the ruined temple.

In the middle ground, between the swineherd and the ruins of Solomon's temple, is a little pyramid, symbol of the precious capstone or corner-stone which once crowned the temple and is destined to do so again when the temple is rebuilt.[10] This is the stone that is so easily rejected or overlooked.[11] It shows two of its faces, one in shadow and the other illumined. Carved on each of these faces is the letter 'A', thus depicting a 'Double A'.

The boar is a primary emblem of the both the Classical and Druidic Mystery schools. The nose of the boar is reputed to bear a resemblance to the letter 'm' or 'M', which is curiously like the 'Double A' ('AA'). Hence, when the boar roots the ground, he is said to imprint the 'Double A' on the earth with every thrust of his snout. Adonis, Apollo's messenger, is represented by the boar, whilst Apollo himself, like Merlin, is a swineherd. Associated with Adonis is Hyacinth, the fifteen-year old youth beloved of Apollo, who was accidentally slain by the sun-god. Apollo changed the slain youth into a flower, and marked the flower and its leaves with his mourning sighs, 'Ai, Ai,' written as the Greek letter *Upsilon* (Y or υ), a symbol of spiritual knowledge or illumination, which corresponds to the English letter 'V' (*i.e.* 'VV', the mirror-image of 'AA').

> 'Thee my lyre, thee my songs, shall ever celebrate; and, changed to a new flower, thou shalt bear an inscription of my sighs. The time too shall come, when a very powerful hero shall be changed into this flower, and his name read upon thy leaves.'

While these things are uttered by Apollo's prophetic mouth, lo, the blood, which falling upon the ground has stained the grass, ceases to be blood, and a flower more bright than Tyrian purple springs up, assuming the same form as the lily, but that in the former is a purple colour, in the latter that of silver. But this is not enough for Phœbus, for he was the author of the honour now bestowed: he marks his own sighs upon the leaves, and the flower has Ai, Ai, drawn upon it in funeral characters.[12]

Bearing in mind that the 'Double A' is a symbol associated with Andreas Alciat, alias Shakespeare's Prospero, then Prospero can perhaps be seen to represent the powerful hero mentioned by Ovid—the new Hyacinth.

Emblem No. XLV of Alciat's emblem book is not the only emblem of note in this extraordinary story. Complementing it is Emblem No. II, entitled '*Mediolanum*' ('Milan'), in which a sow, rather than a boar, is featured. The sow is the ancient emblem of the feminine form of embodied wisdom (*i.e.* Sophia), whose piglets are the 'sons of wisdom' ('s.o.w.').

The original 1546 version of the emblem depicts a sow standing at the foot of an oak tree, but this is changed in the 1564 edition for a picture depicting the city of Milan, in which a temple is being built by freemasons. In the foreground three craftsmen are lowering a 'little sow' into a deep pit. The sow is thus being buried as the foundation sacrifice, on a site where once the cult of Minerva (Athena) was practised. The 1577 and 1584 versions show a similar but redrawn picture. This time, on one of the stones, that has been quarried and is being worked on near the pit, is carved a single letter 'A'. When the 1589 edition of *Emblemata* was published, the same emblem No. II, although seemingly identical to the previous 1577 and 1584 editions, appeared with the letter 'A' removed from the stone. Instead, a border around the emblem picture is introduced, in which a 'Double A' is depicted in a 'head-piece' form.

Ten years previous to this the 'Double A' headpiece had begun to appear in books printed in London by Thomas Vautrollier, Thomas. It first appeared in Thomas Chaloner's *De Rep. Anglorum Instauranda libri decem,* published by Thomas Vautrollier in 1579. This was followed by *The Essayes of a Prentise in the Divine Art of Poesie* of King James VI of Scotland, published by Vautrollier in 1584/5,[13] in which the identical 'AA' headpiece was used as in Porta's original 1563 cipher book, *De Furtivis Literarum Notis.*

Vautrollier, Thomas was the well-known London print-er whose printing shop was in Blackfriars and whose widow married Richard Field, the successor to the printing business. The latter printed *The Arte of English Poesie* in 1589 and *Venus and Adonis* in 1593, both of which carried an 'AA' headpiece. *Venus and Adonis*, the 'first heir' of Shakespeare's 'invention', notably displays the 'VA' sign in the capitals of its title, which would appear to be a deliberate esoteric signature, especially when followed by the 'Double A' device. Adonis signifies Mercury, or the mercurial mind, in this poem, and is the counterbalance and polarity to Venus, the personification of desire. These two, Venus and Adonis (Mercury), represent the Twin Pillars of the Temple of Solomon, between which we have to pass in order to enter the temple of light. In particu-lar, Venus and Adonis signify the bases of the pillars. The two A's crown these pillars. Hence either 'AA' or 'Venus and Adonis' ('VA') signify these Great Pillars.

From these dates onwards many of the finest examples of English literature in the Elizabethan-Jacobean period car-ried the 'Double A' device in one form or another (usually as a headpiece), including Shakespeare's *Sonnets* (1609), the 1st folio edition of the *Authorised Version of the Holy Bible* (1611), the *Genealogies* in the 1st quarto edition of the Scriptures

(1612), and Shakespeare's 1st folio edition of *Comedies, Histories and Tragedies* (1623). But it is the link with Prospero and *The Tempest*, Shakespeare's reputed last play, and with the Rosicrucians, which is so interesting, bearing in mind that Prospero appears to embody a fusion of Prospero Colonna and Sforza, Francisco, Duke of Milan, both of whom were admitted into Parnassus by Apollo and Athena, and Andreas Alciat whose 'signature' is 'AA', and that Shakespeare's signed works began with the 'VA' of *Venus and Adonis*.[14]

All the indications are, therefore, that *The Tempest* is Shakespeare's intended last play and the crown of his work, of which *Venus and Adonis* was the signed beginning or base; and, moreover, that it is a Rosicrucian work, and Shakespeare, the author, was a Rosicrucian.

May this set us free!

Plates

11. 'DOUBLE A' HEADPIECE (SHAKESPEARE'S *SONNETS*, 1609)

12. 'DOUBLE A' HEADPIECE (*THE ARTE OF ENGLISH POESIE*, 1589)

13. 'DOUBLE A' HEADPIECE (BAPTISTA PORTA'S *DE FURTIVIS LITERARUM*, 1563)

Mediolanum.

Bituricis veruex, Heduis dat Sucula signum.
His populis patriæ delita origo meæ est,
Quam Mediolanam sacram dixére puellæ
Terram: nam vetus hoc Gallica lingua sonat.
Culta Minerua fuit, nuc est, vti numine Tecla
Mutato matris virginis ante domum.
Laniger huic signum sus est, animalq̃ biforme,
A cribus hinc setis, lanitio inde leui.

14. THE MILANESE FOUNDATION SACRIFICE
'Mediolanum', Alciat's *Emblemata* (1564).

EMBLEMA XLV.

ROSTRA *nouo mihi setigeri suis obtulit anno,*
  Hæcq̃ cliens ventri xenia, dixit, habe.
Progreditur semper, nec retrò respicit vnquam,
  Gramina cùm pando proruit ore vorax.
Cura viris eadem est, ne spes sublapsa retrorsum
  Cedat; & vt.melius sit, quod & vlterius.

15. 'DOUBLE A' CORNERSTONE AND SOLOMON'S TEMPLE
Emblem XLV, 'In Dies Meliora', Alciat's *Emblemata* (1577).

BIT ᴠ R I G I S *vernex, Heduis dat ſucula ſignū:*
His populis patria debita origo mea eſt,
Quam Mediolanum ſacram dixere puella
  Terram: nam vetus hoc Gallica lingua ſonat.
Culta Minerua fuit. nunc eſt vbi numine Tecla
Mutato, Matris virginis ante domum.
                                    B 2   *Lani·*

16. THE MILANESE FOUNDATION SACRIFICE AND 'SINGLE A'
Emblem II, 'Mediolanum', Alciat's *Emblemata* (1577, 1584).

BITVRICIS veruex, Heduis dat fucula fignum:
  His populis patriæ debita origo meæ est.
Quam Mediolanum facram dixere puellæ
  Terram: nam vetus hoc Gallica lingua fonat.
Culta Minerua fuit, nunc est vbi numine Tecla
  Mutato, Matris virginis ante domum.
Laniger huic fignum fus est, animalá biforme,
  Acribus hinc fetis, ianitio inde leui.

17. THE MILANESE FOUNDATION SACRIFICE AND 'DOUBLE A'
Emblem II, 'Mediolanum', Alciat's *Emblemata* (1589).

Notes on the Text

Foreword

1   Richard de Bury, High Chancellor of England, *A Vindication of [Epic and Dramatic] Poetry* (15th C.).

2   See especially:-

Colin Still, *Shakespeare's Mystery Play* (1921) and *The Timeless Theme* (1936).

W. F. C. Wigston, *The Columbus of Literature* (1892) and *Bacon, Shakespeare and the Rosicrucians* (1888).

Frances A. Yates, *Shakespeare's Last Plays* (1975) and *The Occult Philosophy in the Elizabethan Age* (1979).

Noel Cobb, *Prospero's Island* (1984).

Chapter 1

1   *Henry VIII* was further revised and added to after May 1621, since the play includes details drawn from Sir Francis Bacon's fall from the office of Lord Chancellor, in addition to details concerning Cardinal Wolsey's fall from the same office.

2   The Annual Assembly and Feast Day of the Craft Freemasons is on St John the Baptist's Day, 24 June (Midsummer's Day). The two St Johns are called 'The Grand Originals' and are the patron saints of Freemasonry and Rosicrucianism. Their feast days are referred to as 'The Two Great Parallels', relating to the poles of the year (*i.e.* Midsummer and Midwinter). Freemasons used to be known as St John's Men or St John's masons. Legend explains that St John the Beloved completed, by his learning, what St John the Baptist had begun by his zeal.

3   The 1583 enterprise was led by Humphrey Gilbert. After landing in Newfoundland, they sailed on further south. Eventually all but one ship survived and returned to England.

The 1584 enterprise was led by Sir Walter Raleigh and landed in Chesapeake Bay. Returning to England with glowing reports of the region, the land was named Virginia in honour of Queen Elizabeth. Raleigh returned to Virginia in 1584, to establish a settlement on Ronoake Island under the command of Ralph Lane. The settlers returned with Sir Walter Raleigh in 1586. Another expedition was sent by Raleigh in 1587 to settle Ronoake. The Spanish Armada invasion of England made it impossible to send victuals over to the colonists from 1588-90. When the relief ships did arrive in 1590 the colonists had vanished.

4   In 1910 Newfoundland issued a 6 cents memorial stamp commemorating its 300th Anniversary. The stamp displayed a portrait of Sir Francis Bacon, stating that he was 'the guiding spirit in Colonization Schemes.'

5   Stowe's *Annals.*

6   Part II, Book x.

7   *The True Declaration*, Council of Virginia (1610).

8   Ibid.

9   *Discovery of the Barmudas*, Sylvester Jourdain (1610).

10 *True Reporatory of the Wracke*, William Strachey (1610/1625).

11 The first three decades of *De Nouo Orde* were translated into English by Eden, the last five decades by Lok, and the complete English version was published in 1612. Shakespeare may have had access to the translations before they were published, but it is just as likely that he read the original.

12 'One, among them, the eldest as he is judged, riseth right up, the others sitting still: and looking about, suddenly cries with a loud voice, *Baugh Waugh....* the men altogether answering the same, fall a stamping round about the fire... with sundrie outcries.' (*Purchas His Pilgrimage* [1613], p. 637.)

Notes on the text

¹³ See the excellent notes to the Arden edition of *The Tempest,* edited by Frank Kermode. (6th edition, 1958.)

¹⁴ Frances A. Yates, *The Occult Philosophy in the Elizabethan Age; Giordano Bruno and the Hermetic Tradition; The Rosicrucian Enlightenment; Astraea; Shakespeare's Last Plays.*

Manley P. Hall, *Sages and Seers; Pathways of Philosophy; The Adepts in the Western Esoteric Tradition; The Secret Teachings of All Ages.*

¹⁵ The *prisci theologia* consisted of divinely inspired pre-Christian authors, including Hermes Trismegistus, Zoroaster, Orpheus, Pythagoras, Plato, Philolaus and other Greek authors.

¹⁶ See Peter Dawkins, *Arcadia* (FBRT, 1988).

¹⁷ *Monsieur de Thou's History of His Own Time...* (1730), ed. B. Wilson, vol. II, p. cxxix. (See 'The Impact of Freemasonry on Elizabethan Literature' by Ron Heisler, publ. in *The Hermetic Journal,* 1990.)

¹⁸ See the title page to *The Advancement and Proficience of Learning* (1640), where Francis Bacon is described as being *'Tertius A Platone, Philosophiæ Princeps'* ('The Third after Plato, the Prince/Chief/Leader of Philosophy'). Marcilio Ficino was the Second Plato.

¹⁹ See *Manes Verulamiani*: a collection of thirty-two Latin elegies in honour of Francis Bacon written by scholarly friends and published by William Rawley in April 1626. The 'Tenth Muse' is Pallas Athena, 'the Shaker of the Spear.'

²⁰ Francis Bacon, letter to John Davies (1603) (Spedding 10.65).

²¹ R.P., *Manes Verulamiani* (1626), Elegy 4:-

So did Philosophy, entangled in the subtleties of Schoolmen seek Bacon as a deliverer... He renewed her, walking humbly in the socks of Comedy. After that, more elaborately he rises on the loftier buskin of Tragedy...

²² The Active Science is the sixth and last part of Bacon's *Great Instauration (i.e.* the restoration of the state of paradise, but with

knowledge or illumination rather than the initial innocence or naivety).

23 Frances A. Yates, *The Occult Philosophy in the Elizabethan Age,* 'Christian Cabala and Rosicrucianism.'

24 *The Great Assises Holden in Parnassus by Apollo and his Assessours,* by George Withers (1645).

25 Ben Jonson, tributary poem 'To the memory of my beloved, The Author', Shakespeare Folio (1623).

Chapter 3

1 Virgil, *Æneid*, Book VI, lines 604-7.

2 Ibid.

3 *The Tempest*, II, i, 193-194.

4 *The Tempest*, III, iii, 1-4.

5 This title is derived from the earlier Egyptian story of Isis and Horus, Isis being the widow of Osiris and Horus being her son (*i.e.* the son of the widow Isis). Jesus was also the son of a widow.

6 *The Tempest*, II, i, 78-82.

7 *i.e.* Manannan son of Lir (Irish, Manannan Mac Lir; Welsh, Manawyddan ap Llyr).

8 Pindarus, *Odes*. Quoted by W. F. C. Wigston, *Bacon, Shakespeare and the Rosicrucians* (London: George Redway, 1888), ch 3, p 50.

9 *The Tempest*, II, i, 86-89.

10 *The Tempest*, IV, i, 122-124.

11 *The Tempest*, II, i, 51.

12 Related in *Curious Myths of the Middle Ages* by Baring Gould, 'Fortunate Isles', p. 553.

13 Christine Hartley, *The Western Mystery Tradition*, ch IV (London: Aquarian Press, 1968).

Notes on the text

[14] *The Tempest*, v, i, 17-32.

[15] *The Tempest*, v, i, 78-79.

[16] *The Tempest*, v, i, 130-4

[17] *The Tempest*, v, i, 291-7

[18] *The Tempest*, III, iii, 21-24

[19] Genesis i, 27-28.

[20] Francis Bacon, *Novum Organum,* Bk I, Aph.129.

[21] Francis Bacon, *Advancement of Learning,* The Preface (1640).

[22] *The Tempest*, I, ii, 72-74.

[23] *The Merchant of Venice*, IV, i, 180-198.

[24] See *Genesis* v, 22-24.

[25] See *Hebrews* xi, 5.

[26] *The Tempest*, I, i, 1-5.

[27] *The Tempest*, v, i, 33-57

[28] Ovid, *Metamorphosis*, vii, 197-209.

[29] Jonson, *The Fortunate Isles and their Union*, I, i, 1-8.

[30] *The Tempest*, IV, i, 165.

[31] *The Tempest*, IV, i, 184.

[32] *The Tempest*, v, i, 316.

[33] *The Tempest*, Epilogue, 16-20.

[34] The sidereal cycle of Jupiter is calculated as 11.86 tropical years.

[35] *The Tempest*, I, ii, 274-279.

[36] *The Tempest*, I, ii, 294-6.

[37] *The Tempest*, I, ii, 53-54.

[38] *The Tempest*, II, i, 163-4

Chapter 4

1   *The Tempest,* I, ii: 257.

2   *The Tempest,* I, ii: 296-298.

3   Auriel is also known as *Haniel.*

4   The ancient 24-hour day began with the sunset of the previous day. Thus the night hours were the first hours of the day, which were followed by the daylight hours, just as Darkness precedes Light in Genesis. The Qadosh, therefore, began the day of the Passover, with the Qadosh being held soon after sunset, at the start of the day, and the Passover being celebrated later, in the daylight hours. The Passover, at which the Pashe (Lamb) was eaten, was celebrated standing up, in a hurry, and was a meal involving the family. The Qadosh, on the other hand, was celebrated amongst friends, sitting at a table, during which the Cup of Brotherhood, or Loving Cup, was shared. The Last Supper held by Jesus and his close friends, his apostles, was the Qadosh, and it fell then on a Friday.

5   *The Tempest,* I, ii, 383-389.

6   See Manly P. Hall, *The Secret Teachings of All Ages,* CLVII-CLVIII.

7   Ancient Hebrew has no written vowels.

8   *John* xiv: 10.

9   *The Tempest,* III, ii: 133-7.

10   *The Tempest,* V, i, 88-89.

11   *The Tempest,* V, i, 50-57.

12   Mercury is from the Latin *Mercurius,* which itself is derived from the Ancient Egyptian *Maa Kheru* meaning 'True Word'.

13   *The Tempest,* III, iii: 21-24.

14   Francis Bacon, *Advancement of Learning,* Bk. II, (1605).

15   Francis Bacon, *Advancement of Learning,* Bk. II, (1605).

16   *The Tempest,* I, ii: 189-193.

17 *The Tempest*, I, ii: 242-245.

18 *The Tempest*, I, ii: 247-249.

19 *The Tempest*, IV, i: 48.

20 *The Tempest*, V, i: 4.

21 *The Tempest*, V, i: 17-19.

22 *The Tempest*, V, i: 240-1.

Chapter 5

1   Francis Bacon, *Advancement of Learning*, Bk II (1605).

2   Francis Bacon, *Advancement of Learning*, Bk I (1605). The description is derived from that of Marsilio Ficino, *Arg. ad Hermes Trismegistus*: 'Et philosophus maximus, et sacerdos maximus, et rex maximus'.

3   Francis Bacon, *Advancement of Learning*, The Preface (1640).

4   *The Tempest*, V, i, 205-207.

56 Francis Bacon, *Advancement of Learning*, Bk I (1605):-

    …The essential form of knowledge…is nothing but a representation of truth: for the truth of being and the truth of knowing are one, differing no more than the direct beam and the beam reflected.

7   *The Tempest*, IV, ii, 163-164.

8   See Henry Cornelius Agrippa, *De occulta philosophia*, III, iii (1651).

9   *The Tempest*, V, i, 24-28.

10 *The Tempest*, V, i, 50-52.

11 Shakespeare uses this musical symbol of love's art in several of his plays—*The Merchant of Venice* and *Pericles* being two other prime examples.

12 Matthew vii, 7-8; Luke ix, 10.

[13] Francis Bacon, *Advancement of Learning, Book* I (1605). The allegory is derived from Homer, *Iliad*, viii, 19.

[14] See Francis Yates, *Shakespeare's Last Plays: A New Approach*, ch 4 (London: Routledge & Kegan Paul, 1975).

[15] Luke, xxiii, 34.

[16] John, xiv, 12.

[17] Exodus xxi, 23-25.

[18] Matthew iii, 11.

[19] *The Tempest*, v, i, 28-30.

[20] 1 John iv, 8.

[21] Cabalistically the principle of Beauty is represented by the archangel Michael, whose name means 'Face or Countenance of God'.

[22] *The Tempest*, v, i, 206-207.

[23] Sri Yukteswar, Sutras 1 & 2, *Kailya Darsanam* ('Exposition of Final Truth') translated by Self-Realisation Fellowship, published as *The Holy Science,* by Swami Sri Yukteswar (Self-Realisation Fellowship, Los Angeles, California, USA, 1984).

[24] *The Tempest*, v, i, 206-215.

[25] The Taittirya Upanishad 3. 1-6, from *The Upanishads*, p 111 - Translations from the Sanskrit with an introduction by Juan Mascaro (Penguin Books, 1965).

Chapter 6

[1] I *Corinthians* xiii.

[2] Plutarch, *Vit. Rom.* 28.

[3] *The Tempest*, v, i, 275-6.

[4] The Lesser Mysteries at Eleusis in Greece were further subdi-

Notes on the text

vided into lesser and greater mysteries, the first two stages (earth-water) belonging to the Eleusinian lesser mysteries and the second two stages (air-fire) to the greater mysteries.

5   Ovid, *Metamorphoses*, i, 21.

6   Preface to *Theatrum Poetarum*, Edward Phillips (1675).

7   *Of Atheism*, Francis Bacon (1625).

8   *The Tempest*, II, i: 1-8.

9   *The Tempest*, II, i: 34, 37, 41-42, 45.

10 *The Tempest*, II, i: 48, 51, 56-57, 59-62, 66-68.

11 *The Tempest*, II, i: 109-118.

12 'Blessed are the pure in heart, for they shall see God.' (From Jesus' Sermon on the Mount.)

13 Hence the zodiacal sign of Libra, the Balance, represents the adept in the overall cycle of development. In Libra the perfect balance and harmony of all things is attained. This leads on to Scorpio, in Scorpio's highest sense as represented by the Eagle and Dove symbolism, wherein takes place the Mystery of Mysteries—the Mystery of Death. In Scorpio the great cycle of human evolution ends and the true master is found—the Master of the Zodiac, the Master of the Round Table, the Master of the Wheel of Life, the Lord of Time and Space—He who is truly free.

14 *The Tempest*, I, ii: 12-20.

15 *The Tempest*, I, ii: 26-31.

16 *The Tempest*, V, i: 24-32.

17 II *Corinthians*, iv: 15-17.

18 *Of Adversity*, Francis Bacon (1625).

19 Teachings of a modern master, Peter Deunov (Beinsa Douno), publ. in *Prophet for Our Times*, ed. David Lorimer (Element Books, 1991).

20 Ibid.

[21] *The True Declaration*, Council of Virginia (1610).

[22] *The Tempest*, I, ii, 272-274.

Chapter 7

[1] *The Tempest* II, ii: 186.

[2] *The Tempest* III, ii: 6.

[3] *The Tempest* III, ii: 121.

[4] *The Tempest* III, ii: 124.

> A 'picture', in this context, is an image or thought-form, which is an apt description of Ariel; whilst 'No body' (like 'No thing') is an occult reference to the formless Divine Essence or Spirit of Love.

[5] *The Tempest* IV, i: 205-6.

[6] *The Tempest* IV, i: 239.

[7] *The Tempest* II, i: 177.

[8] *The Tempest* IV, i: 32.

[9] *The Tempest* V, i: 172-5.

[10] *The Tempest* V, i: 200-213.

[11] *The Tempest* V, i: 213-215.

[12] *The Tempest* I, ii: 181-184.

Chapter 8

[1] Edm. Spenser, *The Faerie Queene*, Book VII, Canto VII, verse 59.

[2] Edm. Spenser, *The Faerie Queene*, Book VII, Canto VIII, verses 1-2.

[3] See Peter Dawkins, *The Wisdom of Shakespeare in As You Like It*, ch

6, 'A Walk through the Heavens' (IC Media Publications, 1998).

4   See also Frances Yates, *The Occult Philosophy in the Elizabethan Age*, ch. IX, 'Spenser's Neoplatonism and the Occult Philosophy: John Dee and *The Faerie Queene*' (Routledge & Kegan Paul, 1979).

Chapter 9

1   These three worlds are represented by the alchemical elements of air, water and earth respectively, hence the symbolism associated with these gods and goddesses.

2   Francis Bacon, 'Cupid or the Atom', *Wisdom of the Ancients* (1609).

3   Ibid.

4   Ibid.

5   See Peter Dawkins, *As You Like It*, ch 7, pp 130-132 (IC Media Productions, 1998).

6   'All the fortunate isles' refers to Cyprus (Macaria) and her island colonies that were established by the sons of Macar—Lesbos, Khios, Samos, Kos and Rhodes, known collectively as the Macares.

7   Ben Jonson, *The Fortunate Isles and their Union*, written for Twelfth Night, 1625, but delayed for three days and first shown on Sunday 9 January 1625, with Prince Charles as the chief masquer.

Chapter 10

1   Romans viii, 24.

2   *The Tempest*, III, i, 37-47.

3   *The Tempest*, I, ii, 152-153.

[4]   *The Tempest*, I, ii, 307-308.

[5]   *The Tempest*, I, ii, 17-2 1.

[6]   *The Tempest*, II, i, 110-118.

[7]   *Matthew*, v, 13.

[8]   *The Tempest*, I, ii, 160-7.

[9]   *The Tempest*, III, iii, 40.

[10] *The Tempest*, II, i, 33-45.

[11] *The Tempest*, II, i, 71.

[12] *The Tempest*, II, i, 78-79.

[13] *The Tempest*, III, iii, 110.

[14] Oxford Dictionary.

[15] In Homer's *Odyssey*, bk. xiii, swine are described as being beside the rock *korax*. The sow is a symbol of the goddess and druidess in the Druidic Mysteries, just as the boar is a symbol of the god and the druid. The raven is a symbol of clairvoyance.

Chapter 11

[1]   Francis Bacon, *Advancement of Learning* (1605).

[2]   Francis Bacon, *Novum Organum* (1620).

[3]   Francis Bacon, *De Augmentis Scientiarum* (1623).

[4]   Shakespeare, *The Winter's Tale*, IV, iv, 86-97.

[5]   Shakespeare, *The Tempest*, II, i, 139-165.

[6]   Quotation from 'Of the Canibales' in John Florio's 1603 English translation of Michel de Montaigne's *Essaies*, Bk I, ch 31.

[7]   Ibid.

[8]   Ezekiel was one of those who vigorously attacked the unjust

Notes on the text

assumption that the sins of the father are automatically passed on to the son (Ezekiel xviii).

9   Francis Bacon, *Advancement of Learning,* Bk 2 (1605):-

The unlearned man knows not what it is to descend into himself, or to call himself to account.... The good parts he hath he will learn to show to the full, and use them dexterously, but not much to increase them: the faults he hath he will learn how to hide and colour them, but not much to amend them: like an ill mower, that mows on still and never whets his scythe. Whereas with the learned man it fares otherwise, that he doth ever intermix the correction and amendment of his mind with the use and employment thereof. Nay, further and in sum, certain it is that Veritas and Bonitas differ but as the seal and the print: for Truth prints Goodness; and they be the clouds of error which descend in the storms of passions and perturbations.

10   Preface to *Theatrum Poetarum,* Edward Phillips (1675).

11   *The Tempest,* I, ii, 311-315.

12   *Hell* originally meant 'ice-cold' and 'dark,' being the realm of death in which life (*i.e.* warmth, movement, light) is resisted and stifled. *Hell* is the realm of Matter, the polarity to Spirit, which is Light.

13   See John xxi, 1-14.

14   Francis Bacon, Essay *Of Atheism* (1625).

15   *The Tempest,* I, ii, 374-376.

16   *The Tempest,* II, ii, 140-141.

17   *The Tempest,* III, ii, 133-141.

18   *The Tempest,* V, i: 294-297.

Chapter 12

1   Apollo is the Greek version of St George, being the God of
    Enlightenment who, with his partner, Pallas Athena, Goddess
    of Wisdom, inhabits Mount Parnassus. Mount Parnassus is the
    legendary Mountain of Wisdom and Poetic Inspiration, habita-
    tion of the Muses and the place of the famous Delphic Oracle. It
    corresponds to the symbolism of the Pyramid. Inside the moun-
    tain is coiled the fiery Python, the great dragon whom both
    Apollo and Athena periodically 'slay' with their spears of light in
    order to transmute the earthly energies and qualities, which the
    dragon represents, into a blaze of light and beauty. Apollo and
    Athena are the 'Spear-Shakers', the Rosicrucian archetypes or
    genii. The heroes whom they preside over, and of whom they
    are the patrons, are the Rosicrucian knights, who wear the
    'armour of God'.

2   Shakespeare, *As You Like It*, II, vii, 58.

3   For a discussion of this, see Francis Yates, *The Rosicrucian
    Enlightenment*, ch. 3-4.

4   *e.g. Mathematical Magick*, by Dr. John Wilkins, first Secretary of
    the Royal Society, 1680 edition, p. 237:–

    'Such a lamp is likewise related to be seen in the sepulchre
    of Francis Rosicross, as is more largely expressed in the
    Confession of that fraternity.'

5   See Paul Foster Case, *The True and Invisible Rosicrucian Order*
    (Samuel Weiser, 1985), for an example of the cabalistic symbol-
    ism and cipher.

6   See in particular the introductory notes by F. N. Pryce to the 1923
    SRA reprint of *The Fame and Confession of the fraternity R: C:
    Commonly of the Rosie Cross.* by Eugenius Philaletes (Thomas
    Vaughan).

Notes on the text

7   Theophilus Scgweighardt, *Speculum sophicum Rhodo-Stauroticum* (1618).

8   Andreæ, *Mythologiaæ Christianæ...Libri tres*, (Strasburg, 1618), VI, 13 (p. 290).

9   De Bry, *Icones Virorum Illustrium*, Pt.II, p.134.

10 The temple as a pyramid is referred to in this ancient symbolism, whose capstone is the corner stone that brings all the corners together in a point at the apex.

11 See Psalm cxviii, 22; Ephesians ii, 20; 1 Peter ii, 5-8.

12 Ovid, *Metamophoses*, X, 196.

13 *The Essayes of a Prentise* claims to have been 'Imprinted at Edinburgh by Thomas Vautrollier'; but the fact is that Vautrollier's printing business was in London.

14 See Peter Dawkins, *Arcadia*, Pt II, 'The AA Signature of Light' (FBRT, 1988).

Index

235

The Wisdom of Shakespeare in *The Tempest*

Index

The Wisdom of Shakespeare in *The Tempest*

Index

Index

The Wisdom of Shakespeare in *The Tempest*